REVIEWS FOR OTHER GHOST BOOKS BY TROY TAYLOR

In his nearly three dozen volumes, Troy Taylor has consistently managed to mesh his fervent enthusiasm for historical detail with the anecdotal and investigative evidence finding that has won him thousands of loyal readers. Though properly leaning toward the skeptical, Taylor has never once undermined his own sense of wonder at paranormal events and his deep respect the people who experience them.
URSULA BIELSKI, author of **CHICAGO HAUNTS**

Troy Taylor's HAUNTED ILLINOIS manages to capture the spookiest aspects of life on the prairie in a way that no other book has done. For those who believe that Illinois is merely corn fields and forests, he only needs to read this book to realize that strange things are lurking on the midwestern plains.
DAVE GOODWIN, author of **GHOSTS OF JEFFERSON BARRACKS**

Historians and cavers alike will find a wealth of information contained in DOWN IN THE DARKNESS and Taylor, a caver himself, also recounts stories of lost treasure caves and disputed civilizations underground. There is nothing better than a good cave book when you just can't get underground. This book should help you through those desperate times. Put on your helmet, turn down the lights and enjoy a unique journey into the dark, ghost-infested underworld.
PAUL STEWARD - NATIONAL SPEOLOGICAL SOCIETY NEWS

Troy Taylor has brought a new level of professionalism to the field with the GHOST HUNTER'S GUIDEBOOK, which stands as the best and most authoritative book written to date on ghost investigation. Both beginners and experienced investigators alike should make this book their bible... it gives the straight savvy... the material is grounded, practical and informative. It comes as no surprise that Taylor's book has received international praise!
ROSEMARY ELLEN GUILEY, author of **ENCYCLOPEDIA OF GHOSTS & SPIRITS**

GHOST BOOKS BY TROY TAYLOR

HAUNTED DECATUR (1995)
MORE HAUNTED DECATUR (1996)
GHOSTS OF MILLIKIN (1996 / 2001)
WHERE THE DEAD WALK (1997 / 2002)
DARK HARVEST (1997)
HAUNTED DECATUR REVISITED (2000)
FLICKERING IMAGES (2001)
HAUNTED ILLINOIS (1999 / 2001 / 2004)
SPIRITS OF THE CIVIL WAR (1999)
THE GHOST HUNTER'S GUIDEBOOK (1999 / 2001/ 2004)
SEASON OF THE WITCH (1999/ 2002)
HAUNTED ALTON (2000 / 2003)
HAUNTED NEW ORLEANS (2000)
BEYOND THE GRAVE (2001)
NO REST FOR THE WICKED (2001)
THE HAUNTING OF AMERICA (2001)
HAUNTED ST. LOUIS (2002)
INTO THE SHADOWS (2002)
CONFESSIONS OF A GHOST HUNTER (2002)
HAUNTED CHICAGO (2003)
DOWN IN THE DARKNESS (2003)
FIELD GUIDE TO HAUNTED GRAVEYARDS (2003)
OUT PAST THE CAMPFIRE LIGHT (2004)
THE HAUNTED PRESIDENT (2005)

WEIRD U.S. (Barnes & Noble Press) (2004)
Co-Author with Mark Moran & Mark Scuerman

WEIRD IL (Barnes & Noble Press) (2005)

COMING SOON

DEAD MEN DO TELL TALES (2005)
by Ursula Bielski & Troy Taylor
GHOSTS BY GASLIGHT (2005)
by Troy Taylor & Ursula Bielski

MYSTERIOUS ILLINOIS
ILLINOIS HAUNTINGS

THE HAUNTED PRESIDENT

THE HISTORY, HAUNTINGS & SUPERNATURAL LIFE OF ABRAHAM LINCOLN

BY TROY TAYLOR

- A WHITECHAPEL PRODUCTIONS PRESS PUBLICATION -

... For A Kindred Spirit ...

Original Cover Artwork Designed by
© Copyright 2004 by Michael Schwab &Troy Taylor
Visit M & S Graphics at www.manyhorses.com

This Book is Published by:
Whitechapel Productions Press
A Division of Ghosts of the Prairie
P.O. Box 1190 - Decatur, Illinois - 62525
(217) 422-1002 / 1-888-GHOSTLY
Visit us on the Internet at http://www.historyandhauntings.com

First Edition - June 2005
ISBN: 1-892523-40-X

Printed in the United States of America

The Haunted President
INTRODUCTION

*"Who is dead in the White House?", I asked one of the soldiers.
"The President", was the answer, "he was killed by an assassin."*

**President Abraham Lincoln recalling a dream that
he had a few days before he was assassinated**

Growing up in Central Illinois, Abraham Lincoln was almost a part of my daily life. There was nowhere that I could go and not hear something about him or at least be given some reminder that he once lived literally steps away from the same places that I did. In that part of Illinois, there are towns, streets, highways, businesses, theaters and even taverns that bear the name of Lincoln. The former president became commonplace to most of us and we saw him as little more than a distant icon and forgot that he was once simply a man, a person just like the rest of us.

It was many years after I left my childhood behind that I began to develop an interest in the life and times of Abraham Lincoln - especially his strange and supernatural side. Most people don't know that Lincoln was laughed at by his neighbors when he was a young boy because he had been kicked in the head by a horse. They passed off his odd behavior as the result of brain damage and believed that he would never amount to anything. Most don't realize that Lincoln was a great believer in signs and portents or that he believed in the spirit world.

The connections between Lincoln and the supernatural were maintained throughout his life, and some say beyond it. Much has been made of Lincoln's prophetic dreams and of his belief in the spirits and, of course, of the hauntings which are said to be connected to his home in Springfield, his mysterious tomb and beyond. Many stories have been told of his belief in the spirit world, but why did those beliefs become such a prominent part of his life and what event caused

Lincoln to turn to contact with the dead?

Lincoln was always a melancholy person. The death of his mother when he was still a child, hard labor to make an existence for himself in the wilderness and his struggle for an education, all combined to make him a serious man, even when he was making a joke. The Civil War caused him great sorrow and the heavy losses on both sides filled him with sadness. Lincoln paid obsessive detail to everything about the war and by 1864, portraits of him show a face etched with lines. He slept very little in those years and during the five years he lived in the White House, he spent less than one month away from work. His only escape was afforded him by the theater, by his books or a late night buggy ride.

Lincoln always stated that he longed for a life of peace and contentment, but seemed to also know that he would never live to find it. It's not surprising to learn that legend has it that Lincoln's ghost is one of the most restless in American history but even his life was one of strangeness and mystery.

In the pages ahead, I would like to take the reader along on a trip backward in time in a search for the strange and unusual man known as Abraham Lincoln. These pages will likely introduce you to things that you never knew about our most famous president, and to some stories that you may be familiar with --- although possibly not as they will be presented here. Before reading any further though, the reader should know that I make no claims of being a Lincoln scholar or an expert on his life. I am merely like most of you who picked up this book, a common person who was fascinated by the side of Lincoln that was never presented in our high school history books.

The reader may find this book to be shocking, tragic and sad but will hopefully find it compelling as well. There is much here of mystery, grave robbery, murder, death and general weirdness. In fact, if even some of the stories of Lincoln and the supernatural are true, then he may be the most well-traveled ghost in American history. With all of the ghosts and hauntings associated with Lincoln's life and death, the reader can only imagine that there are many unanswered questions about Lincoln that are left to be explored. Many of those questions will be delved into within these pages.

You will have to decide when you finish if Abraham Lincoln can truly rest in peace. I'll present the evidence of his troubled life, his turbulent term as wartime president, the hysteria and horror of his death, the spirits of his assassination and his ghostly here-after --- and the reader can decide for himself.

Happy Hauntings!
Troy Taylor
June 2005

1. THE EARLY LIFE OF LINCOLN

Abraham Lincoln was born in Kentucky in 1809. His father, Thomas Lincoln, had married Nancy Hanks, a tall, pretty, uneducated girl, three years before and they had built a log cabin at a place called Sinking Springs Farm. Thomas was known as a good man and a good storyteller and one who was adept at many things, although he rarely settled down to try any one thing in particular.

Abraham looked to follow in his footsteps. He was a thin and spindly-looking boy who showed remarkable curiosity about everything. He would toddle into the nearby village of Elizabethtown and watch the travelers of the Cumberland Gap pass by him. He was already much taller than the local children by the age of seven when he and his older sister, Sarah, began attending "blab" school, which meant all of the students read their lessons aloud at the same time. Years later, Abraham would be remembered as being the best reader in school.

The Lincoln family later pulled up stakes and moved across the Ohio River to Indiana, where they settled on Little Pigeon Creek. Abraham soon learned the ways of the outdoors and hard work, helping to clear land around their new home. He became known as an honest and self-reliant boy, but lonely and withdrawn too, sometimes vanishing into the woods for hours at a time.

In 1818, Lincoln's life changed abruptly when the family was struck by a terrible frontier disease dubbed "milk sickness". Tom and Betsy Sparrow, close friends of the Lincoln family, died first, while Nancy Lincoln faithfully nursed them to their last hours. Then, Nancy too was struck down with the disease and followed her friends to their graves. With his own hands, Abraham helped to fashion his mother's coffin and then helped place her in the ground. It was later said that he held his head in his hands and wept for hours. At that point, his father and sister forgotten, Lincoln later said that he felt completely alone in the world.

In 1819, Thomas Lincoln traveled back into Kentucky and returned with the widow of an old friend. Her name was Sarah Bush Johnston and she became his wife and a new mother for Abraham and Sarah. He also brought along Sarah's three children and an orphaned cousin named Dennis Hanks. The cabin was now jammed to capacity with the expanded family and Abraham later recalled escaping into the woods with his books for some peace and quiet.

But no feature of backwoods life pleased Lincoln as much as a trip to the local mill. It released him from a days work in the fields and gave him the opportunity to watch the movement of the mill's primitive machinery. One day, when taking a bag of corn to the mill, he arrived late and his turn did not come until nearly sundown. In accordance to the usual custom, Lincoln hitched his old mare up to the arm of the gear that turned the millstone and got the horse moving. The animal moved slowly and the mill turned at the same speed. At frequent intervals, the boy made use of his whip to urge the animal on. With a careless "get up, you old hussy", he applied the lash with each revolution.

Just as he called out to the horse and lashed it again, the old mare, resenting the feel of the whip, kicked backward and struck Lincoln in the head, sending him sprawling on the ground. Old Man Gordon, who owned the mill, picked up the bleeding, senseless boy, who he believed was dead, and sent for Thomas Lincoln. He came as quickly as he could and loaded the bloody boy into his wagon and drove back home. Abraham lay unconsciousness all night but as dawn began to break, he started to show signs of waking up. He jerked a couple of times and then called out "get up, you old hussy", which had been interrupted by the mare's hoof.

Over the next few days, Lincoln slowly recovered from his injuries, for the most part anyway. Many people who knew him during his Illinois years remembered that he sometimes seemed "in a world by himself", ignoring his surroundings and visitors to his office. He would sit for several minutes in complete silence, staring straight ahead. A few friends described him as rejoining the visitors "like one awakened from sleep" when such an interval ended. In Washington, a number of distinguished foreign visitors noted this strange habit. One French nobleman counted "twenty such alterations" in a single evening.

One of his closest friends and long-time law partner, William H. Herndon, stated that Lincoln was "a peculiar, mysterious man with a double consciousness, a double life. The two states, never in a normal man, co-exist in equal and vigorous activities though they succeed each other quickly."

But Lincoln's strange behavior never stopped him from excelling in school. Lincoln stood out among the other backwoods students. He composed poems

Lincoln's second home, where he lived for five years during his childhood. The photo was taken many years after the Lincoln's moved away (Illinois State Historical Society)

and essays and often mounted a tree stump for speeches on whatever subject took his fancy. He was obviously a born politician, but on the other hand, was also an expert log-splitter, a master with a farm plow and skilled as a hog butcher. He was also regarded as an insatiable reader. He started with the Bible and then read anything he could get his hands on. He was definitely a young man of many contrasts and not surprisingly, was considered a unique and rather odd fellow.

Lincoln's physical strength was also said to be extraordinary. By the age of seventeen, he was nearly six feet tall and could outwrestle anyone in the surrounding counties. He could also best any of them with his mind too. Local teachers and ministers admitted that the young man was better read than they were and that a life of hard labor on a farm would never suit him. Lincoln agreed and dreamed of far-off places and adventure.

He knew that a life of tedious, hard work was not for him. He often worked along the Ohio River, cutting wood and stacking it on the banks for riverboat captains to buy or worked alone ferrying passengers across the Anderson River but when his father rented him out with his axe for 25 cents per day, he started to grow resentful of the life that he felt trapped in. He went about his labors with a book stuck in his back pocket but even this small escape did little to alleviate his boredom.

Thomas Lincoln pulled up stakes once more in the late 1820's and moved his family to a small farm outside of Decatur, Illinois. Abraham stayed with the family until the following Spring, helping his father build a cabin and clear land for a farm. The Lincoln's remained on their farm near Decatur during what became known as the "Deep Snow". The winter of 1830-1831 was a brutal one, hammering the region with periods of snow and ice that piled up to heights of more than four feet. Livestock perished, game became scarce and many local settlers almost died during the fierce storms. This winter would mark Lincoln's second brush with death.

One day, during the winter, young Lincoln made a snowy journey to a neighbor's house to pick up a few bags of grain and some homemade beer. As he was making his way along through the snow, Lincoln fell through the ice and into the Sangamon River. He suffered a severe case of frostbite but managed to make it to the neighbor's cabin, where he spent the next week in bed. He nearly died, the other settlers recalled, but Lincoln pulled through and when warm weather came, he started out on his own for the first time.

An opportunity had come his way and he found work on a flatboat that was hauling farm produce down the Ohio and Mississippi Rivers to New Orleans. At the end of his journey, he found the promise of a new life in the village of New Salem, Illinois.

2. LINCOLN HISTORY & HAUNTINGS IN NEW SALEM

The town of New Salem, which was barely listed on any map when Lincoln came here and only provided a home for about 12 families, began as the dream of two entrepreneurs with visions of a thriving town on the Sangamon River. It would be here that Lincoln could be his own man and he got a job working in a small store. Soon, more stores opened, along with a tavern, a saw mill and a school and it looked as though the dreams of the founders would be fulfilled as steamboats began navigating the nearby river. But none of the dreams of prosperity would ever be realized and as many have pointed out, New Salem strangely came into its own with the arrival of Abraham Lincoln and died soon after he departed.

New Salem was founded a short time before Lincoln finished his work in New Orleans and decided to return to Central Illinois. James Rutledge and his nephew, John Cameron, brought their families to this region between 1825 and 1826 and established themselves along Concord Creek. They had plans to build a mill on this small tributary from the Sangamon River but soon realized that the Concord would not be able to produce the water volume necessary to power the mill. They soon began to search for a more promising location.

On July 19, 1828, Cameron purchased land along the Sangamon River and applied to the Illinois State Legislature for permission to build a dam across the river. The place was known as "Fish Trap Ford" and was where the road from Beardstown to Springfield, the only major road in the area, crossed the river. In anticipation of a favorable response from the legislature, the two men moved their families to the a bluff overlooking the mill site and Rutledge soon converted his home into a tavern, providing food and lodging for travelers on the road.

Permission came from the legislature in January 1829 and work began immediately. Wooden bins were built in the river and local farmers provided wagons and teams to haul thousands of wagons filled with rocks to fill the structures. When the dam was completed, a combination grist and saw mill was constructed on a platform over the river. It was a success from the start and drew customers from miles around. It was later recalled that it was not unusual to see more than 40 horses tethered to the trees on the hillside as their owners waited for their grain at the mill.

Late that year, in the fall of 1829, Samuel Hill and John McNeil built a general store on the hill that was crossed by the Springfield Road. Around that same time, a saloon was built by William Clary above the mill and began dispensing alcohol to the thirsty customers who waited for their orders to be cut or ground.

With the mill, saloon and store already becoming a center of trade for the area, Rutledge and Cameron began to plan their town around them. On October 29, 1829, a town was platted and lots were drawn up with the name of the settlement to be New Salem. The first lot was sold on Christmas Eve and New Salem began to take shape. On Christmas Day, an official post office was established in the Hill and McNeil store and Samuel Hill was named as postmaster.

The two years that followed saw much in the way of growth for the town. Most prominent among the arriving settlers were Henry Onstot, a cooper, the Herndon brothers and Dr. John Allen, a graduate of Dartmouth College. Each man would leave his mark on the small village but none of them so much as a young man who arrived here in April 1831.

Abraham Lincoln's arrival in New Salem was anything but auspicious. Although accounts vary as to what actually happened, most agree that he was part of the crew of a flatboat that hung up on the dame below the village. From the shore, the townsfolk watched as he and the others struggled to save the boat from sinking. Lincoln was described as an "ungainly youth" but despite his appearance, his thinking was obviously quick. He ordered most of the cargo to be unloaded and taken to shore and then moved the rest of it to the stern of the boat. After wading to shore to borrow a wood drill, he opened a hole in the bottom of the craft and let out the water that had gathered in the bottom. When the vessel was free of water, he plugged the hole and the flatboat slipped effortlessly over the dam.

Lincoln did not stay around New Salem for long at this point, but he did return in July and began running a store for Denton Offutt, who had hired Lincoln to journey aboard his first flatboat to New Orleans. Lincoln soon became very popular in the small village and was liked for his sense of humor and his storytelling ability. He was also a hard worker and a powerful wrestler, which earned him many friends and admirers.

Lincoln seemed to be a good man, albeit a simple one, and most would have never predicted that he would join the New Salem Debating Society or that he would persuade the local schoolmaster, Mentor Graham, to lend him books to further his education. Others were not so surprised when Lincoln began considering a career in law and politics. It was as if, one day, the rowdy, fun-loving frontiersman vanished and was replaced by a moody, deep-thinking intellectual with a tendency toward melancholy.

According to stories, it was the death of a young woman that changed Lincoln's life forever. Their ill-fated love affair has become the legend over the years and some believe that it permanently altered the course of Lincoln's life.

When Lincoln first met Ann Rutledge, the auburn haired beauty was being courted by the storekeepers, Samuel Hill and John McNeil. It was McNeil who eventually won the girl's favor and soon they were engaged to be married. However, in 1832, McNeil sold his interest in the store to his partner and made plans to depart from New Salem for a time. Before he left though, he made a startling confession to Ann --- his real name was not John McNeil but McNamar and he had changed it before leaving home because at the time he believed his family would find him and financially burden him. Now that his future in Illinois was assured, he intended to return to New York, retrieve his family and return to New Salem and Ann. Surprisingly, Ann accepted the story and sent McNamar away with a promise to write. For a time, he did send a few letters but eventually correspondence faltered and then stopped altogether.

After sufficient time had passed, Lincoln began courting Ann and, according to many, a love affair quickly blossomed between the two of them. The idea of a law practice was beginning to come to Lincoln's mind and Ann had decided to attend the Female Seminary in Jacksonville. Following her graduation, and Lincoln completing his studies as a lawyer, the two planned to be married --- but it was not to be.

During this time, Lincoln's plans to be an attorney were interrupted by persuasion from friends and locals that he take up politics. He soon decided to run for the state legislature.

His first campaign got off to a good start when he was chosen to pilot the ill-fated Talisman when it attempted to make the trip upriver to Springfield. This steamboat was to be the first to navigate the Sangamon River and many believed that it would open the city of Springfield for a booming river economy. The plan turned out to be a disaster, after the riverboat became stuck in shallow water, and marked the first and last trip that a riverboat would take on the river.

Despite this outcome, Lincoln was never blamed for the fiasco. Then, a short time later, his campaign was interrupted by the Black Hawk War and he ended up serving two months in the Illinois militia. He was delighted when his fellow soldiers asked him to serve as captain, but often complained about there being more mosquitoes to fight than Indians. He was mustered out after the campaign and set out for home, only to have his horse stolen. Lincoln ended up walking most of the way back to New Salem from the Wisconsin border. By the time he arrived, he had only two weeks left to campaign but still managed to carry his hometown and come in eighth out of a field of eighteen.

Lincoln's return to New Salem had brought him other disappointing news. The store where he had been working had closed down, so he took the position of New Salem's postmaster. He took the liberty of reading dozens of newspapers every week before delivering them and soaking up the information they contained. He also became a deputy surveyor and used both jobs as a way to campaign for the legislature again in 1834. He drummed up votes at dances, barbecues, cock-fights and wrestling matches, where he normally served as referee since everyone refused to fight him.

That following November, at the age of 25, he left for Vandalia to serve in the legislature. He was wearing the first suit that he ever owned. It was soon after that his dreams of a life with Ann Rutledge came to a shattering conclusion.

In early 1835, Ann, now understood to be engaged to Lincoln, received word from the long absent John McNamar. Her fiancé had apparently met with unavoidable delays, including his own serious illness and the death of his father and two brothers in New York. His letter to her stated that he was now returning to New Salem for their wedding.

Ann was distraught by this "good news". She loved Lincoln and yet she was honor-bound to marry McNamar and saw no way out of the situation. She continued her preparation for college and as the summer wore on, she nearly completed her studies.

Later that same summer, Ann fell ill with a fever that eventually left her confined to bed. It grew steadily worse until the doctor announced that there was little hope for her recovery. Although the doctor had ordered strict silence and had forbidden any visitors, Ann repeatedly called for Lincoln and he was eventually summoned to the Rutledge farm. Lincoln entered her sickroom and the door was closed behind him. What may have been said during that final meeting will never be known but the family would later recall that when Lincoln left the house, he fell sobbing against a tree in the yard and stayed there for some time.

A day or so after Lincoln's visit, Ann slipped into unconsciousness and never awakened. Her death came quietly on August 25, 1835 and while the family listed the cause of death as "brain fever", others claimed that the young girl died of a broken heart.

It was said that Ann's death drove Lincoln to despair and that he became so distraught that his friend, fearing that he might take his own life, took his pocketknife away from him and watched him constantly for weeks. Eventually, Lincoln recovered but some say that he was never the same again. Ann's death stayed with Lincoln the rest of his life - and perhaps beyond it.

During the turbulent days of Lincoln's love affair with Ann Rutledge, he was also serving as a successful member of the Illinois Legislature in Vandalia, the state's second capital. The city had only served as the capital since 1820 and the first statehouse in town was nothing more than a plain, two-story frame building with a stone foundation. It was located in the center of the square and it was to here that the archives of Illinois were moved from Kaskaskia in December of that year.

Vandalia became a beehive of activity in the months that followed. The General Assembly met and plans were made to build a bridge over the Kaskaskia River east of town, to build several new roads and to make the city a better place to live. The city grew by leaps and bounds, attracting many new settlers who were coming to Illinois. Vandalia became the final stop on the Cumberland, or National, Road that came west from Maryland and thousands of settlers traveled on this route to the area.

When the General Assembly, composed of 14 senators and 29 representatives, met again in a small frame building at the northwest corner of Johnson and Fifth Streets, Shadrach Bond was the governor. Other officers of the state were Pierre Menard, the lieutenant governor; Elias Kent Kane, a New Yorker who had been an attorney in Tennessee and Kaskaskia, the secretary of state; Robert K. McLaughlin, treasurer; and Elijah C. Berry, the auditor of public accounts.

They met in the wooden house until December 1823, when it burned to the ground. Vandalia citizens built a two-story brick building to replace it but it was torn down in 1836 and some of its wood and brick was used in the capitol building that took its place. Local residents raised $16,000 for the construction of the new building and the legislature first convened there on December 5, 1836. Much remained to be completed though and as noted in a letter that Abraham Lincoln wrote to his friend, Mary Owen: "The new State House is not yet finished and consequently, the legislature is doing little or nothing."

Even when the state house was finished, it was still considered very plain. It was not until 1859 that the eight Doric columns were added up front. This building, which was erected with such high hopes, was only briefly used as the capitol for the state. When it was decided to move the capital to Springfield, the Legislature voted to refund to Vandalia the amount of money the city used to construct the state house.

It was originally agreed that Vandalia would be the capital for 20 years but long before that time, the movement of the population was heading to the center of the state. As time for moving the capital drew closer, more and more interest was shown. In 1833, the Legislature submitted the question of the capital's new location to the voters and Alton received the highest number of votes, with Springfield a distant third. No appropriation for moving was made though and when the question came up again, bills for the Illinois-Michigan Canal and other improvements were being considered. By that time, Sangamon had become the most populated county in the state. It had two senators and seven representatives who were called the "Long Nine" because the men all averaged more than six feet in height. Their plan was to obtain the capital for Springfield. Led by Abraham Lincoln, they voted together and were able to convince others to vote with them. The Legislature, with all of its debt, appropriated $50,000 for the erection of the state house if Springfield citizens would raise a matching fund. It was agreed and Springfield became the third capital of Illinois.

When the capital moved to Springfield, the population of Vandalia declined to only about 300 people. Businesses closed and homes were boarded up. With the city's decline, the old state house fell into disrepair. The state gave part of the building to Fayette County to be used as a courthouse but only a portion of it was ever used. One section was turned into a school for a time but soon, broken windows were not replaced and birds and animals roamed freely through the hallways. The building crumbled for decades, until it was purchased by the county in 1889. The brick columns that had been added years before were replaced by iron pillars and a balcony was added. In 1930, after a fire, the cupola was rebuilt and three years later, the state began restoring the building to its former glory. It remains in preserved condition today and is an integral part of old Illinois history.

And while the old state house is rich in history --- it is filled with legend as well.

There are stories that say that Abraham Lincoln once jumped from a high second-story window to keep from voting on a measure before the Legislature and that Stephen Douglas once rode a donkey up the stairs to the upper floor to celebrate a Democratic victory. It was in Vandalia that these two men first met.

At that time, Stephen Douglas, a native of Vermont who had also lived in Ohio before coming to Illinois, was teaching school in Winchester while he studied law. From his law office in Jacksonville, Douglas went to Vandalia to ask the Legislature for the post of state's attorney, which was an appointed position in those days. In 1835, when Douglas was named to the position, Lincoln, who had come to Vandalia in 1834 as a representative for Sangamon County, voted against him. The two men would continue to clash over the years. Douglas had been one of the first suitors of Lincoln's future wife, Mary Todd, and the men would also battle for a hotly contested Congressional seat in 1858 with a series of debates throughout Illinois. But Douglas was always a gallant man and a gracious one. Although historically overshadowed by Abraham Lincoln, he helped shape the destiny of the United States when he split the Democratic Party with his stand against succession and assured Lincoln's election as president in 1860.

Over the years, the state house has gained a reputation for being haunted, but stories never seem to agree as to who the culprit might be. Could it be one of the lingering legends like former governors Ninian Edwards or Shadrach Bond? Or perhaps, as some have suggested, Abraham Lincoln himself? Although the idea that it might be the haunting shade of a young Lincoln at the old capitol building seems a far stretch, there are

A later view of the Illinois State House in Vandalia
(Illinois State Historical Society)

some who have continued this story for many years. Who better to haunt the place than its most famous former occupant? But Lincoln or not, stories maintain that the building is haunted and many have had strange experiences here over the years.

As far back as the 1960's, visitors and tourists at the old State Capitol claim to have heard voices in empty rooms, footsteps pacing back and forth and have also seen glimpses of figures in hallways and in doorways. A second glance finds these specters always disappear from sight, as if they had never been there at all. According to one witness, who visited the state house in 1992, he was walking through the otherwise empty building one day and glanced up to see a tall, thin figure looking down at him from an overhead balcony. Startled, because he was unaware that anyone else was present in the building, he looked again to see the man was gone. He explained to me that he searched through the place but there was no one there. He was so adamant to see who it was because he was sure the man had looked like Abraham Lincoln.

"I thought maybe there was a re-enactor there that day playing a young Lincoln or something," he told me. "He looked just like him, but without the beard. I looked everywhere though and there was no sign of him."

Was it the ghost of Abraham Lincoln? Perhaps it was or perhaps it wasn't -- but this phantom, as well as the others that have been seen, appear to have been men linked to this place in the past. The old state house may be one of those places where Illinois history still echoes into the present.

Lincoln served out his term in Vandalia and in 1836, he was elected again and this time headed for Springfield, where he would also practice law. He had read all of the books required and in March of 1837 passed the exam that made him an attorney. He borrowed a horse and bid goodbye to the dwindling town of New Salem. The citizens had lost all hope of the river bringing prosperity to the town and three years after Lincoln departed, New Salem was a ghost town.

According to author John Winterbauer, the term "ghost town" has a variety of meanings when it comes to New Salem. He has maintained for many years that if there is anyplace in Menard County that has ghosts, it is this small reconstructed village. He has recounted many stories of ghostly lights that burn in windows at night, the eerie face of a woman that peers from the window of the cabin that once belonged to Samuel Hill and even an unidentified ghost that is believed to haunt a cabin that once belonged to the Isaac Burner family. While the identity of this ghost remains a mystery, there is at least one ghost here who is quite recognizable. She is a spirit who seems to have a very good reason for lingering behind at the site of her former home. A small piece that appeared in the Springfield newspaper, the *Sangamo Journal*, for January 25, 1833 tells a tragic story:

TERRIBLE ACCIDENT ---- We learn that on Wednesday last, while Mr. R. Herndon of New Salem was preparing his rifle for hunting excursion it went off, and the ball, striking his wife in the neck, separated one of the principal arteries, and in a few moments she was a corpse. It is hardly possible to conceive the anguish of the husband on this melancholy catastrophe. The community in which he lives deeply sympathize with him in this afflicting event.

The home where this horrific event occurred is located on the edge of the modern day version of New Salem village. The reconstructed cabin belonged to John Rowan Herndon and his wife, Elizabeth, the sister of village schoolmaster, Mentor Graham. She had married John in Kentucky in 1827 and in the spring of 1831, the couple moved to New Salem. Rowan, or "Row" as he was affectionately called, and his brother, James, opened a store in the village the following autumn but the business was short-lived. By that summer, James had moved away and had sold his half of the business to William Berry. Row and Berry did not get along and Herndon later sold his interest in the store to Abraham Lincoln.

Herndon remained in New Salem however until the tragic accident recounted in the newspaper gave him reason to leave. The incident occurred on the morning of January 18, when he was cleaning his gun. As it happened, Abraham Lincoln was at the nearby Rutledge Tavern that morning, helping to repair a broken bed. He needed a certain tool to finish the work and he sent ten-year-old Nancy Rutledge down to Herndon's house to borrow it.

Nancy later recalled: "When I arrived there Mr. Herndon was loading his gun to go hunting, and in getting ready to go out, his gun accidentally discharged, and his wife, who was sitting near talking to me, was shot right through the neck, her hands fluttered for a moment; then I flew out of the house and hurried home and told Annie and Mr. Lincoln what had happened."

Elizabeth Herndon slumped over to the floor and died immediately in a pool of her own blood. Not long after, her husband moved away forced to deal with the haunting rumors that her death might have been anything but accidental. New Salem cooper Henry Onstot recalled the incident many years later and stated that local residents were divided on whether or not Herndon had killed his wife or whether it had been simply an accident. But regardless, he said "he was fooling with a loaded gun and it went off and killed her."

No matter how Elizabeth died, the question remains as to whether or not she ever left New Salem. In recent years, sightings of a woman in an old-fashioned dress --- who promptly disappears --- around the old Herndon cabin have been many. On one afternoon visit, a man and his daughter were walking near the cabin and the little girl claimed to see a woman on the steps, who then vanished. The father never saw the figure but was so convinced by the story that he looked into the history of the house and discovered the dark tale of Elizabeth Herndon. He became convinced that she was the woman that his daughter spotted that day.

A summer volunteer told author John Winterbauer that she saw the ghost of a woman at the far end of the village on two separate occasions over three years. The first time, she was alone and walking down the path from the second Berry-Lincoln Store and saw a woman on the path in front of her. The ethereal figure took a few steps and then blinked out of sight. "Her back was toward me," she remembered, "so I didn't see her face at all... I'm positive she vanished. It was early afternoon and sunny. I'm sure I saw her."

The volunteer saw the woman again some time later but this time she was not alone. She and another volunteer were walking down the path together and again, it was a bright and sunny day. As they were walking toward the Herndon house, her companion pointed to the porch and asked who was working there that day. She looked up to see where he was looking and saw a woman on the porch of the cabin, in full pioneer costume, holding a broom. As the two volunteers drew closer, they realized that they did not recognize the woman as anyone on the staff and wondered who she might be. They decided to walk over and talk to her.

"Before we got close enough," the volunteer stated, "she turned and, I swear, walked right through the shut door!"

The volunteers tried both doors of the cabin but found them to be locked. They peered into the windows but could see no sign of the mysterious woman. Whoever she had been, she had simply vanished without a trace.

The wide variety of ghostly stories told about New Salem, from floating

One of the homes where Lincoln lived during his years in New Salem. By the time of this photo, the town had fallen into ruin and the home stood in a feed lot.
(Illinois State Historical Society)

lights to spectral cold spots and phantom figures, leads many to believe that Elizabeth Herndon does not walk here alone. There is at least one other sub-stantiated ghost that has been spotted here and John Winterbauer believes that he knows this specter's identity. For those who may have guessed it to be Abraham Lincoln, they could not be more wrong! Although Lincoln has been reported in the former village, it seems unlikely that the ghost of a man that some visitors claim to have seen is actually him. Winterbauer believes that this lingering spirit is that of a man who had a closer connection to New Salem than just about anyone else, a pio-neer named Jack Kelso.

Little is known about Jack Kelso, other than that he was a man of many skills but no fixed trade. He hunted the forests, fished the streams and acted as a general handyman around the village. Kelso was well-liked by his neighbors and it was he who introduced Lincoln to the works of Shakespeare and the poet-ry of Robert Burns. He would be remembered fondly in all of the accounts that mentioned him. Thomas Reep wrote of Kelso: "No one at New Salem lived bet-ter than he, nor was any family more forehanded. He led a happy and contented life."

By 1840, the village of New Salem had all but faded away. Kelso headed out in 1841 to Jasper County, Missouri, near Joplin, and then moved again in 1850 to Atchison County, Missouri, where he eventually vanished from history. The last record of him that exists was in 1868 when he acknowledged a deed for some land that he sold.

John Winterbauer believes that Kelso may still roam the forests around New Salem because he loved the place so much. Even after the town was dying, he stayed behind and it was not until the last house was shuttered and the last store closed that he reluctantly departed. But did he return after death?

Many believe so, including a former Menard County teacher, who used to jog through New Salem each day in the early morning hours. One morning, she was passing one of the cabins and spotted a man standing on the porch who was only there for a few moments before disappearing. The cabin that she passed is a unique structure in New Salem. It is a "dogtrot" cabin, which is essentially two cabins joined together by a shared porch. This cabin once belonged to Jack Kelso and his brother-in-law, Joshua Miller, who was the town blacksmith. The two men had married sisters and upon arriving in New Salem, they constructed their home so that the two women could be near one another. They remained together the rest of their lives, moving to Missouri after New Salem was abandoned.

This has not been the only time that a shadowy figure has been seen near the cabin, suggesting that Kelso may still haunt the village. Another sighting was experienced by a man who worked at the park for many years. He claimed to have seen a man wandering about near the cabin, dressed in clothing from the 1830's. The man walked about the yard, seemingly contented, and then disappeared.

John Winterbauer collected another story of Jack Kelso in the summer of 2004. The story was told to him by a retired couple, Jan and Rex, from Jacksonville, who camped at New Salem for a week and liked to stroll through the village just before the park closed at dusk. On the fourth night they were there, they spotted a man in costume alongside the path. He was wearing dark pants, a long white shirt, boots, suspenders and a strange, floppy looking hat. He seemed completely at ease and there was nothing out of the ordinary about him, as many of the volunteers in the village are dressed in similar costumes.

"We got right up on him," Jan recalled, "and Rex nodded and said "good evening', then this man opened his mouth as if to answer but then he was gone. He didn't fade away or anything like that, he just wasn't there anymore."

Winterbauer asked the couple if they could point out the location of this strange encounter on a map of the park. They both agreed that it had taken place just a short distance down the road from the blacksmith's shop --- only a few feet away from the Kelso-Miller dogtrot cabin!

3. HISTORY & HAUNTINGS IN LINCOLN'S SPRINGFIELD

When Lincoln arrived in Springfield, he was already well-known and well-liked. The New Salem wrestler and speaker was respected in the legislature and had made a name for himself in Vandalia. Thanks to this, many people sought him out in his new career as an attorney. While he was always friendly, Lincoln was still introverted and hard to get to know. He made only a few close friends and often described himself as desperately lonely in his new home. His closest friend became Joshua Fry Speed, a local merchant, and the two became nearly inseparable.

Lincoln was a difficult man to get to know for no matter how kind and good-humored he was, he usually kept his true feelings bottled up inside, fearful of letting anyone see his true nature. Speed was the ideal man to break through his new friend's reserve and he had many of the same concerns that Lincoln had, especially when it came to his feelings about finding lasting love and marriage. They talked for many hours at a time, sharing confidences and learning to trust one another in a way that Lincoln gained the best friend that he would ever have in life.

It was at Speed's store that Lincoln began to make his mark on the city that had recently become Illinois' capital. The city was attracting many fine young lawyers and politicians and they often sought out Lincoln, whose name was becoming well-known. According to Joshua Speed: "Mr. Lincoln was a social man, though he did not seek out company; it sought him. After he made his home with me, on every winter's night at my store, by a big wood fire, no matter how inclement the weather, eight or ten choice spirits assembled, without distinction of party. It was a sort of social club without organization. They came here because they were sure to find Lincoln."

At that time, Springfield was a growing city of about 1,500 people but was still cursed with unpaved streets, no sewers to speak of, no sidewalks, and the bane of the city, a pack of wild hogs which had been roaming the streets for more than a decade. Still, the city did manage to have a social circle. One of the members of the city's elite was Ninian Edwards, the son of a prominent politician. His wife, Elizabeth Todd Edwards, was a born matchmaker and delighted in finding husbands for her sisters among Ninian's friends. Her sister, Mary Todd, came to visit in 1839. Mary was described as being "high strung" but was said to have an engaging personality and a quick wit. She became the center of attention among Springfield socialites and had plenty of potential suitors to choose from, including Stephen Douglas, who was the most insistent.

Abraham Lincoln

In December of 1839, during the grand Christmas cotillion, Mary met a young attorney and political hopeful named Abraham Lincoln. They were attracted to each other from the start. Mary's sister soon noted with disapproval that when Lincoln would call, he would sit in rapt attention to everything Mary said. She believed the young man, who the wealthy family considered to be unsuitable, was paying far too much attention to Mary. And Mary seemed to be returning his attentions for a time, but the following year found her still being courted by other men and Lincoln still pining away after her. At the close of the year, he made his decision, he would marry her.

Whether or not Lincoln formally proposed to her or not, Mary promised to become his wife. For some reason though, on New Year's Day of 1841, Lincoln decided to break off the engagement.

Joshua Fry Speed

Some have speculated that Lincoln was intrigued by the idea of marriage, but afraid of it also. He feared his loss of freedom but was unsure that he wanted to live without Mary. His friend, Billy Herndon, noted that Lincoln was acting as "crazy as a loon". He didn't eat, he didn't sleep, he let his work slide and

A young Mary Todd

refused to meet and dine with friends. Another friend, Dr. Anson Henry, suggested that Lincoln take a trip out of town and try to ease his state of mind.

Some time before, Joshua Speed had moved to Louisville, Kentucky and so Lincoln decided to stay with him for awhile. Unfortunately, things were no better here. Speed was also in the midst of a turbulent relationship with a local woman named Fanny Henning. After a short visit, Speed returned to Springfield with Lincoln. He wrapped up his business affairs to move to Kentucky permanently. He would soon be marrying Fanny but he left his good friend with one piece of advice --- either give up Mary for good or marry her and be done with it.

In the Summer of 1842, Lincoln again turned his attentions to Mary Todd. A friend cleverly arranged a surprise dinner so the two of them would meet and it worked. By November, marriage was on Lincoln's mind again. In fact, it was so much on his mind that on the morning of November 4, he and Mary announced they were going to be married --- that evening.

Their friends were in great haste to make the preparations, surprised by the announcement. There was no time for Joshua Speed to travel from Kentucky, so Lincoln asked another friend, James Matheny, to stand in as best man. Matheny would later write that during the ceremony, Lincoln "looked and acted like a lamb being led to the slaughter." While he was getting dressed, his landlord's son asked him where he was going and Lincoln answered, "To Hell, I suppose."

Despite the haste in making arrangements and Lincoln's obvious foreboding, the ceremony proceeded without a hitch and Lincoln was now a husband.

The Lincoln's had their honeymoon at the Globe Tavern, where they lived the first years of their marriage. There was every indication that their marriage was a happy one, despite Mary losing track of her socialite friends and her sister's warnings that her husband was unsuitable. It was not long before they were expecting their first child and Robert would be born just three days short of nine months after the wedding.

Around the time of his marriage to Mary Todd, Lincoln would also become involved in an affair that he would always consider to have been one of the great-est mistakes of his life. In the summer of 1842, the Illinois banking system col-lapsed and state officers were forced to suspend the collection of taxes when it became obvious that citizens were only able to pay them with depreciated or worthless bank notes.

A man named James Shields was then auditor of the state and Lincoln and Mary Todd, who he was then courting, decided to use some sharp wit to poke fun at the Democrats who were running the state. They had singled out one man in particular, the pompous State Auditor, James Shields. In August and September, they wrote a number of letters to the Sangamo Journal that were supposedly written by a fictitious lady named "Rebecca". The letters not only took aim at Shields' financial policies, but questioned his honesty and mocked his manly courage as well. The letters were obviously meant as satire but many of the Democrats, already feeling public pressure, did not take them that way. Shields was enraged. He demanded to know who had written the letters and when confronted, Lincoln took the blame. Shields then sent Lincoln a demand --- that he could both confess to writing the letters and retract them in full, or face "consequences which no one will regret more than myself".

Lincoln didn't bother with it. He thought the whole thing was a silly joke but Shields was not satisfied and soon word spread around Springfield of an impending duel between the two men. Lincoln suggested that the two men fight it out with cow pies, but Shields was having none of it. Lincoln, having no desire to fight Shields, was stunned by the whole thing. Hoping to cool tensions, he sent Shields a letter and offered to confess to writing the letters but only if they could be taken as "political" only and not written in a way to defame Shields' charac-ter. If Shields still wanted to have a duel, then Lincoln stipulated that it must be held with cavalry broadswords while standing on a wooden plank that was 10 feet long and 12 inches wide. Most would agree that Lincoln was not really seri-ous about this, and that his stipulations were actually just to show how ridicu-lous the whole thing was. Others have speculated that Lincoln hoped that Shields would realize that such a duel would have a devastating effect on the smaller man, as Lincoln's blade, with his lanky arms, would have a much longer reach.

Shields still refused to reconsider the idea and he arranged for the two men to meet in Alton and to hold the duel at a place called "Sunflower Island", which was a short distance away from the city on the Mississippi River. Dueling was illegal in Illinois and so by meeting on neutral ground, they would be able to avoid the authorities.

In those days, it was not uncommon for men to settle their differences by dueling. These "affairs of honor" were violent and often to the death. They were carried out covertly, although as long as the fight was considered to be fair, the participants were usually safe from arrest. The quarrels often began in newspaper columns, in speeches, or in off-hand remarks. The duels were seen as a continuation of business or politics and often the negotiations involved in a duel could be more complicated than the quarrel that prompted the affair in the first place.

On the morning of September 22, 1842, Abraham Lincoln and James Shields, along with their "seconds", a physician and a number of friends, met on Sunflower Island, which was near the Alton Ferry landing to St. Charles County and west of the present-day Clark Bridge. Asked to choose weapons, Lincoln, who was much taller than this prospective opponent and with much longer arms, picked up a broadsword and began using it to hack at tree branches that were well out of Shield's reach. With such a vivid demonstration, apologies were renewed between the two men and mutual friends convinced Shields to listen to Lincoln's explanation. The fight was called off but if the duel had proceeded, two promising political careers could have ended. Shields later became a Brigadier General in the Mexican and Civil Wars and a U.S. Senator from Illinois, Minnesota and Missouri. In 1855, Lincoln was a favorite to unseat him in Illinois but Lyman Trumbull defeated them both.

After the matter was settled (at least somewhat - the friends of the two men and their seconds continued to threaten and challenge one another for some time afterward), the party rowed back to Alton, where those who awaited the outcome of the duel had no idea what had transpired. As the boat carrying the group returned to the river landing, many anxious spectators were startled to see a "bloody corpse" on the floor of the boat. One of the women fainted but Lincoln and Shields burst into laughter for the "corpse" was actually just a log that was wearing a red shirt. After the "duel", the parties were hosted at the Old '76 Tavern in town.

And while it seemed that the matter ended on a light note, Lincoln was so ashamed of the affair that he never talked about it again. After that, he never published cruel or embarrassing letters either, even for satire. He also became very opposed to physical violence and when insulted, or if someone tried to pick a fight with him, Lincoln simply laughed and walked away. He would remember how badly things could have turned out for the rest of his life.

By 1844, Lincoln was able to afford to purchase a home in Springfield. It was a one-and-a-half story cottage at the corner of Eighth and Jackson Streets, not far from Lincoln's law office in the downtown district.. The Lincoln's lived in the house from a period shortly after Robert was born until they moved to Washington in 1861.

The house was originally built in 1839 by a Reverend Dresser and was designed in the Greek Revival Style. Lincoln purchased the home in 1844, while it was still a small cottage. It had been constructed with pine exterior boards;

walnut interiors; oak flooring; and wooden pegs and hand-made nails held everything together. In 1850, Lincoln improved the exterior of the property by having a brick wall constructed and by adding a fence along Jackson Street but nothing major was done to the house until 1856. At this time, the house was enlarged to a full two stories, adding new rooms and much needed space.

Today, the house is presented in much the same way as it looked during the Lincoln years. It is now owned and operated by the National Park Service and they are not publicly thrilled that the house has gained notoriety as a "haunted" site. They have always maintained that no ghosts walk here, although many of the witnesses to the strange events have been former employees and tour guides of the house.

For many years, stories have circulated about a tall, thin apparition who has been seen here, accompanied on occasion by a small boy. Many would pass this off to wishful thinking, but in more than one circumstance, the image of Mary Lincoln has been easily recognized. Most believe that if any Lincoln spirit resides here, then it is hers. They believe this house was the one place where Mary was truly happy while she was alive. Is it possible that her spirit may have returned here after her death?

A number of years ago, the Springfield State Journal-Register newspaper interviewed some (then) current and former staff members of the house, all of whom claimed to have had brushes with the supernatural here. At that time, a woman named Shirlee Laughlin was employed at the house as a custodian. She claimed that her superiors were very unhappy with what they termed her "vivid imagination". But were the events she experienced really all in her mind?

In her interview, Laughlin claimed to have experienced ghosts in the house on many occasions. "I don't see the images as such," she said, "I see things happening."

Among the things she witnessed were toys and furniture that could be found in different rooms of the house at different times, seemingly moving about on their own; unlit candles that would mysteriously burn down on their own; and Lincoln's favorite rocking chair rocking back and forth under its own power. "At times, that rocking chair rocks," she stated, "and you can feel the wind rushing down the hall, even though the windows are shut tight."

Laughlin also recounted an occurrence that took place while she was rearranging furniture in Mary Lincoln's former bedroom. Besides being a custodian, she was also an expert on historic home restoration and would often attempt to recreate the layout of the household furniture as it looked when the Lincoln's lived in the house. She was in the bedroom alone one afternoon when someone tapped her on the shoulder. She looked around the room, but there was no one there. She decided to leave the furniture the way she had found it.

And that was not the only weird experience linked to Mary Lincoln. Another anecdote concerned a key which turned up missing from a wooden chest in Mary's room. "We looked everywhere for it," Laughlin reported, "then one morning it just showed up in the lock with a piece of pink ribbon tied to it." No explanation was ever discovered for where the key had been or for who had tied the piece of ribbon around it.

One former guide said that she was on duty at the front door one afternoon when she heard the sound of music being played on the piano that used to be in the parlor. She turned to stop whoever had touched it and found that no one was in the room.

Another ranger who worked in the house recalled several occasions when strange feelings, and the touch of invisible hands, caused her to close up the house quickly on some evenings.

And again, she wasn't alone either. One ranger, who spoke to me anonymously, told me of one late afternoon when she was in the front parlor by herself. There is a display here of some of the items that could commonly be found in households of the period, including some children's toys. As she was standing in the room, she caught a movement out of the corner of her eye. When she looked, she saw a small toy as it rolled across the floor on its own.

She didn't stay in the room very long.

Staff members are not the only ones to have odd encounters. A number of tourists have also noticed things that are a bit out of the ordinary, like hearing voices in otherwise empty rooms; hearing the rustle of what sounds like a period dress passing by them in the hallway; experiencing unexplainable cold spots; and most common, seeing that rocking chair as it gently moves back and forth.

One tourist, an attorney from Virginia, even wrote the staff after he returned home to tell them of his own strange sighting. He claimed to see a woman standing in the parlor of the house who abruptly vanished. He had enough time to recognize her as Mary Lincoln.

Lincoln's love for travel and the law caused his marriage to suffer badly in those early years. At that point in his career, he was active in court cases all over Illinois and was constantly away from home. Mary, left alone with a toddler, was sure that something terrible was going to happen while he was away. Their second son, Eddie, was born in 1846 but only lived to the age of four. Willie followed in 1850, not long after the death of his brother, and Thomas "Tad" Lincoln was born in 1853. The children drew Lincoln closer to home but his marriage was still sometimes rocky. He was nine years older than Mary and almost a foot taller. She often complained that he treated her more like a child than a wife.

Lincoln's law practice was based in Springfield, where most people in Central Illinois had to bring their grievances for settlement. However, twice each year, a judge took justice out to the people. At fixed sessions of two days each week, this special magistrate sat at county seats that were scattered all over the prairie and tried to mete out rulings on the crimes and cases of each locale. Joining the traveling tribunal across what was known in Illinois as the Eighth Circuit, was a band of lawyers who sought out clients at each stop and defended them with skill.

One attorney that could always be found on the circuit was Abraham Lincoln. In those days, few of the county seats could be reached by the new railroads. Most were only accessible by muddy tracks that passed for roads, across bridges that often washed out and along wooded trails that were traversed on horseback. Lincoln usually traveled at the head of the caravan that was made up of the other lawyers and the judge. His long legs made an excellent marker for what streams could be safely crossed by the other men. They slept in farm

Lincoln during his days on the law circuit
(Illinois State Historical Society)

houses and barns and in tavern beds. The courtrooms were primitive and defense strategies often had to be created on the spot.

Lincoln was all business during his trials, listening attentively when not involved in the case, assisting other lawyers with advice and pleading his own cases in the slow drawl that he became famous for, always with care and common sense.

When the official work days ended, the lawyers usually gathered around the fire at the local tavern to play cards, swap stories and sing songs. Lincoln was usually the center of attention, whether he was laughing about the day's activities, telling jokes or participating in mock trials aimed at his fellow lawyers. He also would mingle with the people that he met in the small towns and backwoods communities, visiting their homes, talking about their crops and livestock, discussing politics or bouncing their children on his knee. He was contented with this --- making his living as a carefree nomad, far from the responsibilities of his office and home.

Life continued for Lincoln in this manner for some time. He served a term in Congress in the late 1840's but his law practice kept him too busy to consider much of a political career. It would be the institution of slavery, and his empathy for the people who suffered from it, that would slowly start to alter the course of his career.

Lincoln had been raised in a Baptist family and he knew that his father's decision to leave Kentucky for Indiana in 1816 was at least in part the desire to get the family away from the ugly presence of slavery. In mostly white Indiana and Illinois, Lincoln had little personal experience with black people. The terrifying problems of slave unrest and violence lay far away in states like Virginia and the Carolinas, where slaves had been bought and sold for generations. Illinois' problems were more from ignorance and prejudice and the self-educated Lincoln was not immune to either. He believed, in common with most people at the time, that Negroes were likely by nature inferior to whites, were unfit to vote or to serve on juries and without question, to marry outside of their race. As the perfect subject for crude, frontier humor, Lincoln had no qualms about referring to black men as "boys" or about telling stories that involved "pickaninnies" and "darkies". With his pioneer origins, it is amazing how far Lincoln evolved on the subject of race in the years ahead but his journey was slow to begin.

In 1828, at the age of 19, Lincoln brought a cargo of produce down the Mississippi to New Orleans and witnessed black slave markets for the first time. He was unimpressed with such a sight at the time but gradually, his feelings changed and by the time that he was 28, he and his friend Dan Stone became the only state legislators in Illinois to take a stand against slavery. The men called it an "injustice" and condemned the lynch mobs that terrorized blacks and abolitionists. But they had also gone on to condemn "abolition doctrines" as well, stating that they increased rather than abated slavery's evils. Lincoln was content to believe that slavery would eventually die out on his own and while he hated the institution, he did not endorse its abolishment. Instead, Lincoln was opposed only to the further spread of slavery in the country and was content with the Missouri Compromise, which outlawed slavery in the west, where America's future would be built.

But in 1854, a congressional act, provoked by Lincoln's long-time personal and political rival, Stephen Douglas, threatened to allow slavery in the territories. Lincoln's anger at this got the best of him and he made the decision to largely abandon his law practice and get back into the political arena.

In the Summer of that year, Lincoln decided to campaign for a seat in the Illinois State Assembly. He easily won the position, but then quickly resigned. What he really wanted was a seat in the U.S. Senate, where he believed he could really make a difference for his country. In February 1855, he sought but failed to get the coveted seat. Things started to change in early 1856 however, as a new political party was created called the Republican Party.

The "Little Giant" Stephen Douglas
(Illinois State Historical Society)

The first political move by the party was to try and keep Democrat James Buchanan out of office. They failed, but were gaining attention.

Buchanan's term in the White House pushed back the anti-slavery movement by years. During his time in office, the U.S. Supreme Court ruled in the Dred Scott case, effectively deciding that blacks would never be considered as American citizens. Passions were beginning to ignite in the nation and dire predictions began to be made about the possibilities of secession and Civil War.

Also at this time, Stephen Douglas stepped forward with an abrupt turnabout and announced that he was now totally against allowing slavery into the western territories. Despite his new platform, Illinois Republicans were unconvinced and in June 1858, nominated Lincoln to run against Douglas for a seat in the Senate.

That night, in a speech before the excited nominating convention, Lincoln made his famous "House Divided" speech, declaring that the country could not endure as a divided nation. It was a speech that had been months in the planning and is one that has endured for nearly a century and a half.

On July 24, Lincoln proposed that the two opponents meet in a series of debates before audiences all over the state. Douglas agreed and the two began a series of appearances that have become legend in Illinois for their volatile content. "The prairies are on fire," wrote one reporter, after witnessing a clash between Lincoln and Douglas.

The debates were bitter and powerful between the two long-time rivals. Lincoln argued that slavery must be abolished, while Douglas insisted that it could be contained and allowed to flourish in the South, as long as the states there wished it. The final debate was held in Alton and the story was reported in newspapers all over the country.

By the time the two men arrived in Alton on October 15, 1858, the debates had been raging for some four months. During the campaign, Lincoln had followed Douglas in speaking on 23 of 80 days, and there were six actual debates before Alton. Douglas had traveled more than 5,277 miles of muddy back roads and had made 130 speeches. Lincoln had traveled 4,350 miles and had spoken 63 times. When they came to Alton, Douglas was worn down and his voice was failing but Lincoln's harsh tenor was clearer and stronger than ever.

The candidates arrived in Alton at dawn on the morning of the debate. They came from the river aboard the steamer City of Louisiana and first went to the Alton House, Douglas' headquarters, which was located at Front and Alby Streets. A committee of local Republicans then escorted Lincoln to the Franklin House (later re-named the Abraham Lincoln Hotel). Mary Lincoln and son Robert joined him later that day and the family had dinner and then spent the night at the hotel. Both of the hotels were filled with supporters for the two men and many prominent citizens from Alton and the surrounding area were present when the debate got underway.

The event was held on the east side of Alton's new city hall. The building had been hastily readied for the debate but actual construction would not be completed until 1874. By prior agreement, no slogans or banners were allowed on the podium but the streets and buildings around the site were decorated with signs of support for both Douglas and Lincoln. The estimated crowd of between 5,000 and 10,000 that gathered that day were mostly Democrats though, turning out to support Stephen Douglas. He spoke first, his voice obviously worn down and failing, repeating his stand that it was the right of each individual state to do as it pleased on the question of slavery. He spoke on other issues as well but this subject was a lightning rod of controversy between the candidates. Lincoln argued that the fundamental difference between his supporters and those who supported Douglas was whether or not slavery was wrong. Lincoln repeated his prior statements and belief that a house divided against itself could not stand and that all of the states must be all slave or all free. He believed that a crisis was approaching that would make the country move in one direction or another.

Lincoln was described by the reporters present, as well as the casual listener, as a powerful public speaker. His enemies often painted a portrait of him as a gangling, backwoods lawyer but even the most cynical admitted that he came to life when behind the podium. Francis Grierson, one of many who heard Lincoln speak in Alton, was astonished that "the moment he began to speak, the ungainly mouth lost its heaviness and the half-listless eyes attained a wondrous power." Grierson later wrote that there was something "elemental and mystical" about Lincoln as a public speaker and as a result: "Before he had spoken 20 minutes, the conviction took possession of thousands that here was the prophetic man of the present."

Lincoln may have amazed the audience that was present that day, and may have even won the debate, but he managed to lose the senatorial election to Douglas. Surprisingly, this loss was the best thing that could have happened to him. Wise political analysts, on both sides, had watched this race very closely and had seen the way the debates had captured the attention of the entire country. Soon, word among the Republicans began to favor Lincoln as their choice for President in 1860.

Lincoln began to travel all over the country, backed by the Illinois Republican contingent, making his name known and becoming a recognizable entity. He became so well known in fact that in May 1860, he earned the Republican nomination for President during the party's convention in Chicago.

But Lincoln's nomination almost did not come about and there are many who are still pondering the mystery as to how a minor contender in the presidential race managed to achieve a sweeping victory with the third nomination ballot. The convention was held at Chicago's "Wigwam" and Lincoln's supporters, who had fashioned the man with the image of the backwoods rail-splitter, were thrilled that the event was held in Chicago. The city was not far from being a frontier town itself and Lincoln had many friends and much newspaper support on the Illinois prairie.

The Republicans were holding what was only their second national convention and for the first time, had a chance to usher one of their candidates into power. The dominant Democratic Party was split over the issue of extending slavery into the territories and their divided vote gave the Republicans hope. Coming into Chicago, the favorite to win the nomination was New York senator William H. Seward and his supporters and delegates were so assured of his victory that they focused more on his choice of running mate than on his actual nomination.

The convention opened on the morning of Wednesday, May 16 and over 10,000 people packed into the Wigwam, while an additional 20,000 stood outside. Four years earlier, in Philadelphia, the Republicans had drawn no more than 4,000 people to their convention. The meeting was called to order and was followed by a stirring address from David Wilmot of Pennsylvania. After that, the remainder of the day was spent electing a chairman and constructing a platform. The platform was adopted and modified on Thursday, with the first ballot scheduled for later that evening. Many expected Seward to be chosen by a landslide, so a chorus of groans greeted Chairman George Ashmun when he announced that the printers had failed to deliver the tally sheets. Since no vote could be taken, a motion was adopted to adjourn until Friday.

Lincoln's campaign manager, David Davis, was thrilled. He and his compatriots, who included Lincoln's long-time friends Ward Hill Lamon, William H. Herndon and Stephen T. Logan, saw the delay as a sign from God. Led by Lamon, a number of Lincoln's friends began scrawling the names of convention officers on admission tickets while Norman B. Judd, a railroad attorney, arranged for special trains to bring more Lincoln supporters to the city.

While Lincoln's men worked behind the scenes, Seward's followers publicly declared their man the winner and even put a brass band into the streets on Friday morning. They marched from their hotel to discover that the Wigwam was so crowded that few people other than delegates were able to find seats. Bogus tickets that had been passed out by Lincoln's men had been used so well that the hall was now packed with supporters of Lincoln.

The first roll call of the states gave Seward 173.5 votes, but 236 were needed to win. Lincoln followed with 102 votes, with Simon Cameron of Pennsylvania, Salmon P. Chase of Ohio and Edward Bates of Missouri each receiving about 50 votes. Recognizing that Pennsylvania would be crucial in winning the nomination, David Davis arranged for delegates of the state to be seated between Illinois and Indiana, which both strongly backed Lincoln. He then convinced the delegates from Pennsylvania that if Seward won the nomination, the party would lose the election. As a result, Cameron withdrew.

When the second ballot was tallied, it offered a stunning surprise, especially to the supporters of Seward. Their candidate had only gained 11 votes but Lincoln's total had increased by 79. That left Chase of Ohio on third place with 42.5 votes.

Workers in the Lincoln campaign had been busy contacting delegates from every state, using a deceptively simple strategy. Instead of asking for votes on the first ballot, they persuaded as many men as possible to make Lincoln their second choice. They also stressed the contrast between Lincoln and Seward. Lincoln had been guarded in his campaign so far and had been careful not to offend anyone. Seward meanwhile, had made his position clear on most national issues. Seward was the only nationally known Republican who had allegedly praised John Brown's recent attack on Harper's Ferry and had hinted at a civil war by warning that an "irrepressible conflict" seemed to be coming because of slavery. Lincoln, on the other hand, was on record as opposing the extension of slavery into the territories but he also underscored the conviction that slavery where it existed was lawful and that it should not be challenged. He believed that the institution would die out on its own.

It was obvious that there was a sharp contrast between the familiar candidate with often controversial views and the little known rival who was not nearly as well known or so eager to enter into war, but the contrast was not enough to allow Lincoln to win on just those merits. Lincoln's managers seemed to be willing to promise almost anything to those who would back him. Legend has it that Lincoln sent a telegram to Davis from Springfield that instructed him to make no bargains. "Make no contracts that bind me," Lincoln allegedly wrote and it has been said that Davis used that message to show to those who hesitated in backing Lincoln that the candidate was not offering positions in his administration with a free hand. Legend tells otherwise though and stories have since been told that Davis managed to persuade delegates to abandon their favorite candidates with promises of positions in Lincoln's cabinet.

Whatever happened in Chicago's smoke-filled rooms remains a mystery though. What we do know is that when the third ballot was taken, Seward had lost 4.5 votes and now needed 56 to win. Lincoln however had gained 53.5 votes and was within 1.5 votes of the nomination. The interior of the Wigwam became nearly deafening with the mingled shouts, cries and laughter of the assembled party. And as soon as he could be heard above the commotion, David K. Carter of Ohio jumped up and shouted that five of the delegates from the Buckeye State wanted to switch their votes over to Lincoln! When the commotion subsided again, other states began to call for Lincoln as their new nomination. After all of the 466 votes had been cast, Lincoln had 364 of them -- 128 more than the number he needed to win!

But how did Lincoln manage to pull off such a sweeping victory? Did his campaign managers really trade positions for votes? No one knows and nothing was ever documented that said for sure either way. Journalist Charles H. Ray, a member of Lincoln's inner circle, later said that the managers promised Indiana and Pennsylvania anything and everything they asked for. Carter of Ohio, who started the dramatic third-ballot uprising, is said to have been promised a high level cabinet position and while other rumors abound, nothing has ever been proven.

One thing is clear though. Many who stepped aside for Lincoln, or who worked for him behind the scenes, were chosen for important posts. Seward was made Secretary of State; Chase received the Treasury Department portfolio; Cameron became Secretary of War and the fourth contender for the nomination, Edward Bates, became Lincoln's attorney general. David Davis had hoped to become a federal judge and was appointed to the U.S. Supreme Court in 1862. Ward Hill Lamon, who created all of the bogus tickets, became marshal of the

District of Columbia. William P. Dole, who was credited with securing the Indiana and Pennsylvania votes, was named commissioner of Indian Affairs. And the list went on...

The news of Lincoln's nomination was greeted by skepticism in some quarters but when news reached Springfield, it was immediately greeted by a 100 gun salute. That evening a huge crowd gathered at Lincoln's home and he spoke to them from the front steps, inviting as many into the house as could crowd inside.

Outside of Illinois, Lincoln was not greeted so warmly. Many saw him as nothing more than a "country lawyer" and a "huckster". Even the abolitionists saw Lincoln as a losing figure in the Presidential race and one even declared he was nothing but a "half-horse, half-alligator", bemoaning the fact that he was a backwoodsman from Illinois and Kentucky.

By the summer of 1860, the nation's attention was focused on Springfield and politicians from all over the country were traveling to the city to size Lincoln up. He had become a very real threat to the southern politicians because should Lincoln carry the election, they saw the damage that he could do to their way of life and to the institution of slavery. Many of them came to Springfield to discuss issues because Lincoln's advisors suggested that he remain at home during the campaign. He had others traveling the country and speaking on his behalf. Lincoln was told that this way he could just focus on the issues, but in reality, it was to keep him hidden away. While the Republican leaders had great faith in Lincoln as a candidate, they hesitated to let the public see his lanky frame in his wrinkled suits, frumpy hat and sweat-stained shirts. He was not exactly the picture of a future president, they decided.

The city of Springfield had a carnival-like atmosphere about it that year, highlighted with a Republican rally at the fairgrounds in the heat of the season. The parade took more than eight hours to pass the Lincoln home and ended with a picnic, where tubs of lemonade and whole cooked steers awaited the revelers.

Election day in the city dawned with rousing blasts from a cannon, with music and contagious excitement. Lincoln spent the day and evening with friends at the telegraph office. By midnight, it was clear that he had been elected President of the United States. A late night dinner was held in his honor and then he returned to the office for more news. Guns fired in celebration throughout the night.

Lincoln may have won the day, but he fared poorly in the popular vote. He had soundly defeated Douglas in the Electoral College, but had won just 40 percent of the vote among the people. He had become a minority president with no support at all in the southern states. The current president's cabinet was filled with secessionists and their strong words were starting to be heard among more than just the politicians in the South. Lincoln was even hanged in effigy on

Election Day in Pensacola, Florida.

The country truly seemed to be coming apart.

Lincoln finally managed to return home in the early morning hours although news of victory and telegrams of congratulations were still being wired to his office. He went into his bedroom for some much needed rest and collapsed onto a settee. Near the couch was a large bureau with a mirror on it and Lincoln stared for a moment at his reflection in the glass. His face appeared angular, thin and tired. Several of his friends suggested that he grow a beard, which would hide the narrowness of his face and give him a more "presidential" appearance. Lincoln pondered this for a moment and then experienced what many would term a "vision" --- an odd vision that Lincoln would later believe had prophetic meaning.

He saw in the mirror, that his face appeared to have two separate, yet distinct, images. The tip of one nose was about three inches away from the tip of the other one. The vision vanished but appeared again a few moments later. It was clearer this time and Lincoln realized that one of the faces was actually much paler than the other, almost with the coloring of death. The vision disappeared again and Lincoln dismissed the whole thing to the excitement of the hour and his lack of sleep.

Later on that evening, he told Mary of the strange vision and attempted to conjure it up again in the days that followed. The faces always returned to him and while Mary never saw it, she believed her husband when he said that he did. She also believed she knew the significance of the vision. The healthy face was her husband's "real" face and indicated that he would serve his first term as president. The pale, ghostly image of the second face however was a sign that he would be elected to a second term --- but would not live to see its conclusion.

Lincoln dismissed the whole thing as a hallucination, or an imperfection in the glass, or so he said publicly. Later, that strange vision would come back to haunt him during the turbulent days of the war. It was not Lincoln's only brush with prophecy either. One day, shortly before the election, he spoke to some friends as they were discussing the possibilities of Civil War. "Gentlemen," he said to them, "you may be surprised and think it strange, but when the doctor here was describing a war, I distinctly saw myself, in second sight, bearing an important part in that strife."

Lincoln spent the remainder of the year in Springfield, growing a beard and preparing for the move to Washington. His daily mail, which secretary John Nicolay carried into the office by the basket load, was starting to be liberally sprinkled with hate letters. He was concerned, but never seemed to let it bother him. Lincoln appeared every afternoon in a room at the Capitol building and met with the people, talking and laughing and feeling as though he were still one of them. This went well for some time, but the crowds never seemed to stop coming, so Nicolay cut down the visiting time to only an hour or so each day. Lincoln was becoming exhausted and was starting to worry about the future.

Mary went east to New York in January and her delayed plans prevented her from being home until the night of the last open house in their Springfield home. By this time, their belongings had all been packed away and their steamer trunks had been moved to the Cherney House, a local hotel, to await their departure. Two weeks earlier, Lincoln had traveled to Charleston to say goodbye to his elderly step-mother, and now his farewells were complete.

Lincoln bid goodbye to Springfield on a rainy morning in early 1861. He rode alone in his carriage to the train station. Mary and the boys would meet him in Indianapolis. Lincoln requested that there be no public demonstration over his departure, but several hundred friends and well-wishers lined the streets near the station anyway. His voice was thick with emotion as he said farewell and then boarded the train. He didn't look back --- never realizing that he would never see his beloved city again.

4. WAR COMES TO WASHINGTON

Lincoln's life was already in danger when he departed Springfield. His mail had already started to contain hate letters and death threats. Washington was crawling with rumors that Lincoln was going to be assassinated when he arrived. Reports came to General Winfield Scott that Southern rebels planned to seize Washington, block Lincoln's election and kill him. There was also the danger that someone might kill Lincoln during his trip east. The worst danger seemed to be in Baltimore, where gangs of men were calling for Lincoln's head. The threats were starting to be taken very seriously by the men who vowed to protect the new president and William Seward, Lincoln's new Secretary of State, and General Scott took great care in mapping out Lincoln's train route across America's volatile landscape.

Lincoln's family joined him for the twelve-day journey to Washington, boarding the train in Indianapolis. Unfortunately, not even the presence of his wife and children prevented disaster from almost striking several times. One assassination attempt was averted when guards discovered a grenade in a satchel near the president's seat.

The train traveled across the country to New York, where newspapers and critics mocked Lincoln's awkward gestures and western mannerisms, and then south through New Jersey to Philadelphia. The family checked into the Continental Hotel, where the nearly exhausted Lincoln surrendered to another crowded and noisy reception. Late that evening, Chicagoan and friend Normal Judd called Lincoln to his rooms for a secret meeting with Allan Pinkerton, another Chicagoan and the head of the detective agency who now worked for the Philadelphia, Wilmington and Baltimore Railroad. A short, bewhiskered man with a Scottish burr, Pinkerton informed Lincoln that his detectives had uncovered a well-organized plot to assassinate the president-elect in Baltimore, a rabid secessionist city. Lincoln was scheduled to change trains there and the plotters intended to kill him as he took a carriage from one station to another. Pinkerton and Judd insisted that Lincoln foil the plot by leaving for Washington that night.

But the stubborn frontiersman refused, pointing out that he had promised to speak at Independence Hall the next morning and in Harrisburg the following afternoon. Still, if they really believed that he was in danger, he would try to get away from Harrisburg in the evening. "Whatever his fate may be", Lincoln told him, he would not alter his plans completely. Lincoln then retired to his room to try and rest.

No sooner had he fallen into bed than a knock came at the door. It was William Seward's son, Frederick, with a letter from the Secretary of State and General Scott. The letter warned that there was definitely a plan to kill Lincoln in Baltimore and that he had to avoid the city at all costs. Frustrated, Lincoln realized that he had no choice but to heed the warnings and make plans to do something he hated to do - to sneak into Washington, terrified of being killed by his own people.

The next day, which was Washington's Birthday, Lincoln spoke at Independence Hall and then departed for Harrisburg that afternoon. On the train, Judd took Lincoln aside and rehearsed a clandestine getaway plan that Judd had worked out with railway officials and trusted military officers. At dusk, a special train would spirit Lincoln back to Philadelphia, where he would be ushered in disguise aboard a sleeping coach. A night train would take it to Baltimore and then another would take it to Washington in secret. In the morning, the regular Presidential train would go on to Baltimore as scheduled, with Judd and a military escort on board to protect Lincoln's family and traveling companions.

Again, Lincoln hated the idea of sneaking into Washington but decided to "run no risk where no risk was required" and he went along with Judd's scheme. The only demand that Lincoln made was that Mary be told of the plan. She learned of it that afternoon and was understandably upset. She considered it her right and duty to travel with the president and to stand by his side in case of danger. She realized that she could not in this case but tearfully demanded that Lincoln's close friend Ward Hill Lamon accompany her husband. Mary knew that she could count on Lamon to protect Lincoln with his life.

That night, disguised in a large hat and an overcoat, Lincoln waited for the train in a carriage in Philadelphia. Lamon waited with him, armed with two revolvers, two derringers and two large knives. A Pinkerton agent arrived and escorted him to the train. The sleeping car, which was much too short for the gangly Lincoln, was reserved under a false name, supposedly for an invalid who was being accompanied by his sister. The "sister" was in reality a Pinkerton agent named Kate Warne. It was an inauspicious arrival into Washington, but at least Lincoln was safe and alive.

Lincoln reached the capital at dawn on February 23 and went straight to the Willard Hotel. He had not slept at all and his first view of Washington as the president-elect could not have cheered his heart. Looking out over the city from the carriage that he rode in, he saw only scenes of cold desolation. Down on the bank of the dirty Potomac River, he saw a white shaft of marble against the horizon. It was the unfinished monument to Washington, which looked toward the uncompleted dome of the Capitol Building. Scaffolds covered the cupola and cranes stretched over the dome. There were stacks of building material all around the Capitol and the unfinished Treasury Building. Washington was filthier than Lincoln remembered, with stinking livery stables and rancid saloons at every corner. Pigs rooted in the dirt streets off Pennsylvania Avenue and sewage swamps lay just steps away from the White House. Not far away, near land strewn with garbage, was an open drainage ditch "floating with dead cats and all kinds of putridity", wrote one visitor, "and reeking with pestilential odors." Even now, in the early morning hours, Lincoln noted the foul reek that hung over the city. It was the worst that Lincoln could recall.

Lincoln soon arrived at the hotel, a castle-like structure that boasted of running water in every room, and he checked into a suite, where he and his family would stay until the inauguration. Inside, Lincoln found a letter waiting for him: 'If you don't resign, we are going to put a spider in your dumpling and play the Devil with you." This statement was followed by lines of obscene abuse and ended with "you are nothing but a goddamn Black nigger."

Mary arrived with the boys that afternoon, still shaken from her ordeal in Baltimore, where frenzied crowds had greeted the Presidential train and had shouted for Lincoln. No violence had broken out but Mary had been terrified. She collapsed at the hotel with one of her legendary headaches and did not stir again until late in the evening.

The opposition press noted with sarcasm that the Republican President had arrived without fanfare. And when details of the secret arrival leaked out, papers of all persuasion mocked Lincoln without mercy and published scathing cartoons about the "flight of Abraham". It was the beginning of a merciless smear campaign against the "backwoods President" and his "boorish" wife. Their taunts about his crude behavior and illiterate education wounded Lincoln badly but he never replied to journalistic abuse, writing it off as part of the job. Mary, however was mortified and permanently wounded. She had been from a proud and cultured family, with impeccable manners, and was also very proud of her gifted and intelligent husband. Her hurt and her anger was intensified when the leading ladies of Washington began to snub her, as if she were truly the country bumpkin the papers claimed she was. She became determined to prove she was the best First Lady that Washington had ever seen. She would dress better, furnish the White House better and entertain better than any of the Washington ladies could ever hope to do. She did not realize at the time that such plans would backfire on her and she would never earn the place in Washington society that she so desperately craved.

Inaugural week was a nightmare for Lincoln. For one thing, the rabid and persistent office seekers refused to leave him alone and in addition, the endless delegations from the office of outgoing president James Buchanan and his cabinet filed in and out of his hotel suite. Lincoln was also plagued by groups of congressmen and senators who harassed him about his Cabinet choices and his policy of dealing with the South.

There were delegations from Virginia and the border states as well. One group came from the Virginia secession convention, wanting to see what Lincoln would do and whether they should secede or adjourn. The Virginians urged Lincoln to give them a "message of peace" to take home with them but he would only say that Southerners would be protected in all of their legal rights. Another delegation, consisting of border state Union loyalists, told Lincoln that he must avoid coercion at all costs. He must evacuate Fort Sumter, whose Union flag aggravated the situation with the secessionists, and that he must offer "satisfactory guarantees" to the eight slave states still loyal to the Union. Seward had assured the border Unionists that the crisis would disappear within 60 days of Lincoln being in office but the delegation now wanted assurances from Lincoln himself. Lincoln was blunt with them. He would, he told them, support a slave amendment for loyal states in the Constitution but he would never guarantee slavery in the territories. He also refused to give up any of the military forts the Union held in the south but unknown to the border delegation, he did make an offer to the group from Virginia. He told them that if they could persuade the Virginia secession convention to disband, he would give up Fort Sumter. But the Virginians refused his proposal. All they could promise was devotion to the Union and so both groups departed with no solutions in sight.

Somehow, in the midst of all of the commotion that week, Lincoln managed to complete his cabinet,

William Seward
(Illinois State Historical Society)

even with rival factions hassling him down to the last appointment. It was during this time that Lincoln had his first problem with William Seward. After Lincoln ignored his suggestion for the appointment of Postmaster General, Seward submitted his resignation on the eve of the inauguration. Lincoln was unsettled and realized that Seward, believing himself to be a greater politician than the new President, hoped to try and gain control over the Cabinet and the Administration itself. He reasoned that Lincoln, unable to do without Seward's superior abilities, would offer to remove his choice from the cabinet and replace him with the man his Secretary of State wanted. But Lincoln told his assistant, John Nicolay, that he couldn't "afford to let Seward take the first trick" in their struggle for administrative leadership. Lincoln soon had a confidential chat with Seward and hinted that he might appoint someone else to take his place. Seward quickly withdrew his resignation and Lincoln took "the first trick".

Regardless, the two continued to clash. As Inauguration Day approached, Lincoln carefully crafted his speech. A lot was at stake and Lincoln polished and rewrote with great care. On March 3, he asked Seward to look it over and he returned with the advice that Lincoln should offer greater concessions to the South. He insisted also that Lincoln remove one offensive sentence, which stated that he would recapture all of the federal forts and arsenals that the rebels had already taken over. Lincoln had long been arguing that this needed to be done but Seward convinced him to cut it so that he did not alienate the Southern Unionists, on whom much depended. Lincoln did so, but he would not concede much else. In his mind, the future of freedom depended on him to stand firm. He had been freely and fairly elected and had not lied in any of his pledges to the people who voted for him and his party. If the Southerners did not like him, they were free to vote him out of office in 1864. But they had no right to separate the Union and he was not going to let them. The Union was the authority of the land and could not be wrecked by some disaffected minority. The principle behind secession was one of destruction and no government had ever been established that allowed for its own demise. Lincoln was not going to see the government that he loved be destroyed.

The day of the Inauguration was a grim one in Washington. Heavy storm clouds hung low in the sky and soldiers marched through the crowded streets of the city, ever watchful for the trouble that some said was coming. There were assassination rumors still in the wind and for all of those who feared for Lincoln's safety, there were many others who hoped for terror to strike.

That morning, Lincoln stayed in his suite at the Willard Hotel. He read his inaugural address to his family and then asked to be alone for awhile. When the clock chimed noon, he dressed in a new black suit and stovepipe hat and departed for the lobby. President Buchanan called on him for the traditional carriage ride to Capitol Hill but the two men said little to one another during the journey. The clouds had lifted over Washington and the sun was now brightly shining over the grand parade of horse-drawn floats and military bands. Doubles files of cavalry rode along the flanks of the carriage and lines of infantrymen filed along behind. Hundreds of other officers had been deployed by General Scott throughout the crowd, guarding against assassination. They mingled with the sidewalk crowds and sharpshooters peered over rooftops on both sides of the avenue. As Lincoln looked out over the throng, his eyes landed on the soldiers and he was dismayed to ponder that it was as though the country was already at war.

The carriage pulled up to the Capitol steps and thousands of people surged about the East Plaza, where an enormous platform extended from the buildings east wing. Pinkerton detectives stood about, watching for any signs of trouble and soldiers watched from the windows of the Capitol and from the rooftops of adjacent buildings. On a nearby hill, artillerymen manned a line of cannons, prepared to rake the streets with deadly fire at the first sign of assassins.

Lincoln filed out onto the giant platform with about 300 dignitaries. With a brisk wind blowing, he stood at the podium and looked out over the sea of faces below. Then, he unrolled the manuscript that contained his speech, perched a pair of steel-rimmed spectacles on his nose and began to read in a nervous but clear voice. He spoke at length to the concerns of the Southerners and assured them that he would not endanger their property, their peace or their personal security. He would not menace the institution of slavery as he had, according to the Constitution, no right to do so. But Lincoln also spoke about the supremacy of the national government and vowed to enforce federal law in all states. The Union was perpetual, he said, and could not be destroyed and he promised to shed no blood in its defense--- unless forced to do so. He would, he vowed, "hold, occupy and possess" those southern forts still in Union possession.

Despite these proclamations to use whatever force necessary to save the Union, Lincoln went on to say: "We are not enemies, but friends. We must not be enemies. Though passion may have strained, it must not break our bonds of affection. The mystic chords of memory, stretching from every battlefield and patriot grave, to every living heart and hearthstone, all over this broad land, will yet swell the chorus of the Union, when again touched, as surely they will be, by the better angels of our nature."

Lincoln then turned and faced Chief Justice Roger Brooke Taney and took his oath as the Sixteenth President of the United States. Up on the hill, cannons fired into the wind and a cheer went up from the assembled crowd below. Lincoln had triumphed, it seemed, but little did he know that as his words echoed out over the audience that day, America was beginning the most troubled period in its entire history.

On March 5, with Southerners condemning Lincoln's inaugural address as nothing short of a declaration of hostilities, the War Department sent the President a horrifying report from Major Robert Anderson, the commander of Fort Sumter. The garrison was now surrounded by rebel guns and Anderson had grave doubts as to whether or not he could hold Sumter at all. His supplies were running out and would be exhausted in six weeks. He also feared that any attempt to relieve his men would require a force of at least 70,000 soldiers.

Lincoln was disheartened by the news. He was assured by the War Department that Anderson's opinions could be trusted but Lincoln had no idea what to do. He was no military man and had never commanded anything beyond a company of rough frontiersmen during the Blackhawk War. He felt inadequate to assess Anderson's situation, so he called on General Scott for his opinion. Scott was the General in Chief of the army, a hero of the Mexican War and a professional soldier, despite his elderly years. He suffered from dropsy and vertigo and was so feeble that he could no longer mount a horse or even climb the White House steps without assistance. However, he was a Washington fixture and a legendary soldier which Lincoln had great respect for.

Scott immediately gave his opinion. He believed that it was too late to save Fort Sumter and that Lincoln would be wise to let it go. However, the President was loath to do so and so he spent the next several days consulting with his Cabinet Secretaries and with high-ranking officers in the Army and Navy. The men argued and deliberated and several finally agreed that to try and reinforce the garrison would be disastrous. Sumter had to be surrendered. The situation in Charleston, with rebel batteries lining the harbor and troops and politicians crowding the city, was so dangerous that an aggressive move by the government would be sure to ignite a civil war. Others argued that this would be a grave mistake and Lincoln himself had continued to state that he would never surrender the fort. Would he now go back on his word to the people who elected him to office?

Lincoln was unable to make a decision and so he was forced to wait. He demanded written opinions from the Cabinet and from his generals and then realized that he couldn't depend on any of them to make up his mind for him. He had to decide for himself and on the night of March 28, he locked himself in his office and stayed up all night, pacing the floor and muttering to himself.

Finally, as dawn broke across the sky, he made a decision. He informed his Cabinet that he would dispatch a supply fleet to Fort Sumter and leave it up to the rebels whether to start a civil war or not. That same day, he told the War and Navy Departments to start outfitting a relief expedition for Charleston harbor.

All of the members of Lincoln's cabinet, except for Seward, supported Lincoln's decision. Seward, thanks to promises that he had made to the new Confederate government, was in a desperate dilemma. He had promised them, along with the Virginia Unionists, that Sumter would be abandoned. Yet now Lincoln was insisting that he was going to hold the fort. This "prairie lawyer", who had taken away the nomination and the Presidency from Seward, was rejecting his council and threatening to destroy the negotiations that Seward had privately undertaken. Seward complained that this incompetent had "no relative ideas and no concept of the situation". Consequently, on April 1, he sent Lincoln a memorandum with some thoughts for the President's consideration.

Seward wrote that after one month in office, the administration had no policy, either foreign or domestic. Since the Union faced disaster without a policy, Seward offered one for Lincoln to adopt. First, the government must assure the public that slavery was not an issue in the present situation. The matter concerned union or disunion and slavery must be left out of it. Second, the government must abandon Fort Sumter. This policy then must be pursued energetically by the President or "by some member of his Cabinet" --- in other words, by Seward himself. After that, all debate had to stop and everyone in the administration had to agree with the policy and execute it without question.

Needless to say, Lincoln was appalled by the letter. The Secretary of State was not only criticizing Lincoln but was offering to take over the administration and run it for him. Lincoln wrote Seward a harsh reply but never sent it. Instead, he took him aside in private and told him what the policy of the administration was going to be. Furthermore, it would be Lincoln who would carry it out. Seward found that Lincoln could be tough when pushed too far. "Executive force and vigor are rare qualities," Seward wrote to his wife soon after the incident. "The President is still the best of us."

On April 4, Lincoln directed that Assistant Navy Secretary Gustavas Fox command the Sumter expedition and sent him on his way with three warships, a gunboat and a steamer containing 200 soldiers and a year's worth of provisions. He also sent a special messenger to inform Major Anderson that a relief fleet was on its way.

On April 13 though, telegraph messages about Fort Sumter came in rapid sequences to the White House. The Confederates, who felt betrayed by the false promises that had been made to them by Seward, had opened fire on Sumter the day before and were pounding the garrison with harbor guns. Then came more news --- the rebels had allowed Fox to evacuate Anderson and his men. The brief fight was over and Fort Sumter had fallen.

On April 14, with an air of solemn resignation, Lincoln announced to his Cabinet that the rebels had fired the first shots, forcing on him the decision of "immediate dissolution, or blood". The Union would not fall, Lincoln repeated, and therefore, he would mobilize a militia of 75,000 men to suppress the rebellion and call for Congress to convene in a special session on Independence Day. Officially, Lincoln announced that he would not view the conflict as a war between the states but as an insurrection against the government. Since secession was constitutionally illegal, he refused to concede that any of the states had left the Union. Rather he contended that rebellious citizens established a false, Confederate government that Washington would never recognize. Lincoln's objective now was to suppress the Southern rebels as quickly as possible and restore order in the sections of the country they had seized.

The following day, Lincoln's call for 75,000 militiamen went out to the states and it forced those in the North and the South who had been undecided before to choose sides. In the border states, secession conventions sprang into action, for the thought of invading armies from the North, attacking rebels and freeing slaves was more than even the Southern Unionists could stand. On April 17, the Virginia convention adopted a secession ordinance that was approved by the voters . Virginia joined the Confederacy and the rebels moved their capital to Richmond. Within the next two months, Arkansas, North Carolina and Tennessee also seceded and became Southern states with Maryland, Missouri and Kentucky threatening to go as well.

War had come to Lincoln's very doorstep and the country was coming apart.

In the days, months and years that followed, the personality of Abraham Lincoln was altered considerably. Although he had long been prone to moodiness and "spells", his periods of reflection became longer and more pronounced. As the death toll of the war mounted on both sides, Lincoln became more and more obsessed with God and his divine plan for America - and for the President himself. Lincoln became convinced that he had been born to guide America through the War Between the States. His leadership during this period, although often questioned, never faltered and the events of the early 1860's both strengthened and destroyed the man that Lincoln was.

The great loss of life and the bitter turmoil of the war took their toll on him. He changed and he became more bitter and dark. Gone was the humorous man who was apt to take off his shoes during staff meetings to "let his feet breathe". In his place was a sad, gloomy leader who was prone to severe depression. It was as if the weight of the entire nation had fallen on his shoulders.

Lincoln's times of prayer and contemplation became much longer and he seemed to turn inward. He spoke more and more often of the "hand of God" in certain battles and it was almost as if an uncanny perception somehow strengthened as the war raged on. By this time, Lincoln had truly taken on the mantle of America's military commander. Few realize today just to what extent Lincoln actually orchestrated the Union Army during the bloodiest points of the war, enduring complaints and barbs by ineffectual generals about his "meddling". The inexperienced soldier who had looked for help from his Cabinet members and his aging generals was gone and had been replaced by a Commander in Chief who sometimes claimed supernatural insight into events that were occurring hundreds of miles away.

Documents of the War Department contain one occasion when Lincoln burst into the telegraph office of the department late one night. He had visited earlier, looking for the latest news, but when he came back, he was in a panic. He ordered the operator to get a line through to the Union commanders. He was convinced that Confederate soldiers were just about to cut through the Federal lines.

The telegraph operator asked where he had obtained such information and Lincoln reportedly answered, "My God, man! I saw it". He had been dozing in his office, he stated, and the vision had been sent to him in a dream. Much to the telegraph operator's surprise, a return message that was sent to him some time later informed him that Lincoln's vision had been true. When soldiers in the field asked him where he came by such knowledge, the operator was unable to provide them with an answer that he thought they would believe.

5. THE DEATH OF WILLIE LINCOLN

" Do you ever find yourself talking with the dead? I do... ever since Willie's death. I catch myself involuntarily talking to him as if he were near me..... and I feel that he is!"

Abraham Lincoln, speaking to the Secretary of the Treasury, Salmon P. Chase

The war took a terrible toll on President Lincoln but there is no doubt that the most crippling blow he suffered in the White House was the death of his son, Willie, in 1862. Lincoln and Mary grieved deeply over Willie's death. Their son Eddie had passed away a number of years before and while they didn't know it at the time, Tad would only live to be age 18. This left Robert as the only Lincoln son to see adulthood. Lincoln was sick at heart over Willie's death and it was probably the most intense personal crisis in his life. Some historians have even called it the greatest blow he ever suffered. Even Confederate President Jefferson Davis expressed condolences over the boy's death.

Perhaps the greatest solace that Lincoln received from the perils of the war was his cherished sons, Willie and Tad. As the war dragged on, Lincoln found them to be one of his only antidotes to the depression and anxiety of his position. He treasured the moments that he could spend with them, when he could forget about the bumbling of his generals and the bickering politicians and relax with his sons, reading them stories and sharing their wild fun and antics. He loved to beleaguer his visitors with tales of his "two little codgers" and bragged about them to all who would listen.

Both Willie and Tad found the White House to be a place of constant revelry and Lincoln let them run wild with very few restraints. They ran and shouted in the corridors and burst into Lincoln's office in the middle of conferences, chasing one another through the room and darting in between stiff politicians who were not amused. Tad, who instigated most of the mischief, once aimed a toy cannon at a Cabinet meeting and also liked to stand at the front of the grand staircase and collect a nickel "entrance fee" from those who came to see the President. Also, with Lincoln's help, the boys converted the White House lawn into a zoo, with animals consisting of ponies, kittens, white rabbits, a turkey, a pet goat (which often slept in Tad's bed) and a dog named Jip, who had a habit of sleeping in Lincoln's lap during meals. When the boys were not chasing animals through the Executive Mansion, they were holding fairs and minstrel shows in the attic. One day, Tad discovered the White House bell system, which had cords running to various rooms so that Lincoln or the staff could summon servants whenever they needed anything. Tad set all of the bells clanging at once, sending the White House into bedlam. It took a few minutes, but eventually members of the staff climbed into the attic and found Tad yanking all of the bells and giggling madly.

Inspired by the martial atmosphere in Washington, the boys waged mock battles with neighborhood children on the White House lawn. They also held military parades through the corridors of the house, with the boys and their friends marching in a single line, blowing on old horns and banging tin drums. They carried out secret missions on the White House roof, hiding out and watching for "rebs" with their telescopes.

On another occasion, they held a solemn court martial for a soldier doll named Jack, found him guilty, shot him for desertion and buried him in the White House garden. One day though, they burst into Lincoln's office during a meeting and explained in a breathless voice that they had shot Jack for desertion and buried him but that the White House gardener wanted the doll removed because they had dug up some roses. So, they wanted "Paw" to fix up a pardon for Jack. Lincoln said that he reckoned that he could do that and took out a piece of official stationary. "The Doll Jack us pardoned by order of the President" and signed it "A. Lincoln".

Because the boys loved the Army, Lincoln often took them along when he went to visit General George McClellan's camps across the Potomac. They looked up to the soldiers with wide-eyed reverence and watched the marching bands and the drilling regiments in awe. When Lincoln was presented to the troops, the boys rode with him in his carriage and tipped their hats to the troops just as their father did.

In spite of how it sounds though, life for the Lincoln boys was not all play. The younger Tad was a nervous boy, like his mother, and a hyperactive child with a speech impediment. He was slow to learn and many did not believe that he could read. Mary hired tutors for the boys but Tad had "no opinion of discipline" and teacher after teacher resigned in frustration. But Lincoln refused to worry about Tad, insisting that he would learn his letters over time. The boys might be a little spoiled but he was determined to let them have as much fun as they could. They would have to grow up far too soon already.

In contrast to Tad, Willie had a very serious side and often behaved like an adult. He had turned 11 in December 1861 and many of the Lincoln's friends and staff members commented on his precociousness. The young man would sit in church, listening to the minister with rapt attention while Tad played with a jackknife on the floor of his mother's pew. When he was tired of romping with this younger brother, Willie liked to lock himself in Mary's room, where he would curl up in a chair and read a book or write stories on a

Willie Lincoln

writing pad, just as his father used to do when he was growing up. He also kept scrapbooks about historical and significant events, filled with clippings on his father's inauguration, the war and deaths of important people. Willie was much like his father in so many ways and because of this, was his father's special favorite. He and Willie shared many interests, especially reading, humor and a love for animals. Lincoln had bought Willie a pony for his birthday and it became the pride of the boy's life. Mary loved Willie's gentleness and he was so affectionate that she often counted on him desperately for family companionship. He would, she prayed, "be the hope and stay of her old age."

Tragically, this was not meant to be.

By Spring of 1862, the tide of the war was slowly starting to turn for the Union. Lincoln's generals were finally starting to triumph on the battlefield. Buell had actually managed to defeat the rebels in a battle in eastern Kentucky and Halleck had finally come alive and had sent a column down the Tennessee River. Neither man was cooperating as Lincoln had directed but at least they were fighting. Then came even better news. A Brigadier General named Ulysses S. Grant had driven into northwestern Tennessee and had captured Fort Henry on the Tennessee River and then had stormed Fort Donelson on the Cumberland. He pounded the garrison until it met his terms of unconditional surrender. Lincoln and Stanton congratulated one another when they read the news and Lincoln noted happily that Grant and many of his men hailed from Illinois. Subsequent reports also maintained that Grant's victories had broken the Confederate line in Kentucky and forced the rebels to retreat into Tennessee. Though Halleck, who was sitting behind a desk in St. Louis, claimed most of the credit, Lincoln himself nominated "Unconditional Surrender" Grant for a promotion to major general. After a long and dismal winter, Grant alone had given the president something to look forward to.

While Grant was busy hammering the river garrisons in Tennessee, both Willie and Tad became sick. The onset of their sickness occurred during the last days of January 1862. The boys were out playing in the show and both developed a fever and a cold. Tad's illness soon passed, but Willie seemed to get worse. He was kept inside for a week and finally put into bed. A doctor was summoned and he assured Mary that the boy would improve, despite the fact that Willie's lungs were congested and he was having trouble breathing. Day after day passed and Willie grew more and more sick. He developed chills and soon his fever spiked out of control. White House secretaries later told of hearing his cries in the night.

The reports of what Willie actually died from vary from story to story. In the end, it remains a mystery. He was said to have been a delicate child, despite his rough play with his brother and his outdoor activities. Like his brother Eddie, he may have suffered from "consumption" or according to some accounts, he contracted either an acute malarial infection or typhoid. In either case, the lack of proper sanitation was likely a factor. During this time period, Washington had open sewers and a filthy canal for drinking water. The city garbage was dumped into the water just a short distance from the White House.

Before the boy had taken sick, the Lincoln's had planned a large reception with over 800 people in attendance. The lavish party included dinner and martial music and the invitations had already gone out, leaving Mary no opportunity to cancel. The evening turned out to be a dismal affair for the worried parents as they continually took turns climbing the stairs to check on Willie.

His condition did not improve. The doctor was summoned back and by then, everyone in the household and the offices knew that Willie was seriously ill. More doctors were called in to consult and soon, Willie's illness made the newspapers. The reporters conjectured that he may have contracted bilious fever. One parent stayed with the frightened and sick boy at all times and a nurse came to spell them from one of the local hospitals. After a week of this, Mary was too weak and exhausted to rise from her own bed but Lincoln never left the boy's side, sleeping and eating in a chair next to his bed. All he could do was to bathe his face with a wet cloth and look on helplessly as his son's life slowly slipped away. The doctors had no hope for the child as he grew worse. Soon, his mind wandered and he failed to recognize anyone, including his beloved father.

Death came for Willie on the afternoon of February 20, 1862. Lincoln covered his face and wept in the same manner that he had for his mother years ago. He looked at Willie for a long time, refusing to leave his bed side. "My poor boy," the President is reported to have said. "He was too good for this earth. God called

52

him home. I know that he is better off in heaven, but then we loved him so. It is hard.... hard to have him die."

Mary collapsed in convulsions of sobbing and her closest confidante, her black seamstress Lizzie Keckley, led her away to comfort her. After Mary had departed, Lincoln managed to stand and find his way to John Nicolay's office and then sobbing, walked to Tad's room. He laid down with the boy and tried to tell him that Willie would not be able to play with him anymore; that his brother had died. Tad refused to believe it for a time and then he too began to cry.

Orville Browning, Lincoln's long time friend from Illinois, and his wife, Elizabeth, immediately came to the White House when they heard the news. Elizabeth stayed with Mary throughout the night and Orville began taking care of funeral arrangements. It was a tragic time in the White House and according to the tradition of the day, the mirrors in the house were covered and the mansion was draped in black. The Lincoln's hardly stirred from their rooms. If not for their friends and Lincoln's most trusted staff, the White House would have come to a standstill.

On February 24, a minister conducted the funeral in the East Room, while Willie lay in a metal coffin in the nearby Green Room. It was said that the boy only appeared to be sleeping as his friends and family passed slowly by him, their faces twisted in grief. Lincoln stood with Robert by his side but Mary did not attend the funeral. She was in such a state of shock that she was unable to leave her room. Most of official Washington was there, including Seward, who wept openly, Lincoln's Cabinet and dozens of politicians and George McClellan, who was so moved by the President's suffering that he later sent Lincoln a compassionate note expressing his sorrow and thanking him for standing by him during failure after failure on the military front. When the service was concluded, pallbearers and a group of children from Willie's Sunday school class carried the coffin outside and to the waiting hearse.

The day of the funeral was a stormy one, as if the forces of nature reflected the anguish in the Lincoln's hearts. The procession to the cemetery was several blocks long and it ended at Oak Hill Cemetery in Georgetown. Throughout the day, rainstorms wreaked destruction upon the city. Steeples had fallen from churches, roofs had been torn form houses, trees and debris littered the roadways, and even the funeral procession cowered under the torrents of rain. But as soon as they reached the cemetery, the storm passed over and the air became silent, almost as in deference to Willie Lincoln.

The service was short. Willie had been embalmed to make the trip back to Springfield and be buried beside his brother, but Lincoln changed his mind about that at the last minute. He accepted an offer made to him by a friend, William Thomas Carroll, to place the body of Willie in one of the crypts in the Carroll family tomb. This would be until Lincoln retired from the presidency and returned to live in Springfield himself. He could not bear the idea of having Willie so far away from him just yet.

In fact, Lincoln returned to the cemetery the next day to watch the body as it was moved from the cemetery chapel to the crypt itself. The tomb was located in a remote area of the cemetery and was built into the side of a hill. It was a beautiful and peaceful spot but Lincoln wouldn't be able to leave his son unattended there for long.

Word got out that Lincoln returned to the tomb on two occasions and had Willie's coffin opened. The undertaker had embalmed Willie so perfectly that everyone said he just seemed to be sleeping. The President claimed that he was forced to look upon his boy's face just one last time.

Three years later, the undertakers would remove Willie's body from the vault one final time and transport it to a funeral train which stood ready for departure. The funeral car, draped in black, was divided into three sections. One was for the honor guard, while the other compartment held the body of Willie's slain father. Together, they would make the long-delayed journey back to Springfield.

After the funeral, Lincoln tried to go on about his work, but his spirit had been crushed by Willie's death. One week after the funeral, he closed himself up in his office all day and wept. It has often been said that Lincoln was on the verge of suicide at this point, but none can say for sure. He did withdraw even further into himself though and he began to look more closely at the spiritual matters which had interested him for so long.

6. LINCOLN & THE SPIRITUALISTS

Although many Lincoln scholars say otherwise, it is more than possible that Abraham Lincoln didn't just believe in the supernatural, but that he actually participated in it through séances and attempts to contact the spirit world. Many have scoffed and said that Lincoln had no time for ghosts and spirits, but there are others who say that he actually attended séances, which were held in the White House. Whether he accepted the idea of spirit communication or not, it is a fact that many Spiritualists were often guests there. Several of them were even said to have given him warnings about the dark shadows that hung over his life.

Of course, Lincoln himself was convinced that he was doomed and adopted a very fatalistic attitude during his presidency, especially after Willie's death. After the boy died, Lincoln treasured small items and drawings given to him by Willie, sometimes putting them all over his desk while he worked, hoping to capture his essence. Small toys that had belonged to Willie were placed on his fireplace mantel, along with a framed picture of Illinois. Lincoln would tell visitors that it had been painted by "my boy, who died." His friends stated that Lincoln would often watch the door while he worked, as if expecting the boy to run through it and give his father a hug, as he often did in life.

Willie's death left a permanent hole in Lincoln's heart. Often he would dream that Willie was still alive and would see the boy playing in the leaves on the White House lawn and calling out to him --- only to awaken in his darkened bedroom and realize that it was only a dream.

Lincoln also began to speak of how Willie's spirit remained with him and how his presence was often felt in his home and office. Some mediums theorized that Lincoln's obsession with the boy's death may have caused Willie's spirit to linger behind, refusing, for his father's sake, to pass on to the other side.

Even if Lincoln did become involved with Spiritualism, as so many have claimed, he largely avoided them in public. However, after Willie's death, Mary embraced them openly. This is not surprising with the atmosphere that existed in the White House at that time. The President managed to escape from his despair with work, even though his moments with Mary and Tad tended to bring back his pain again. Tad, who until his brother's death thought life was nothing more than a game, now broke into bouts of crying because Willie "will never speak to me any more." But it was Mary who seemed to be more affected by her son's death. Always high strung and emotional in the best of times, she suffered what was likely a nervous breakdown and she shut herself in her room for three months. She took to her bed, broke into fits of weeping and begged Willie to come back to her. Lizzie Keckley would later recall how tender President Lincoln was with his anguished wife but he worried about her as well, fearful that she would lapse into insanity. One day, he took her to the window of her room and pointed out to a distant structure where mental patients were confined. "Try and control your grief," he told her, "or it will drive you mad and we may have to send you there."

With care from her husband, and Lizzie's friendship and kindness, Mary began to slowly improve, although the mention of Willie's name or a reminder of him would send her into violent sobs. Unable to bear any memory, she gave away all of his toys and anything that might recall him. She never again entered the guest room where he died or into the Green Room where he had been laid out in his coffin. She canceled all but the most important social functions and lived in veritable seclusion, trying anxiously to hold on. Five months after her son's death, she was still so shaken that she could barely write to her friends in Springfield about "our crushing bereavement". Sometimes, she wrote, when she was alone, she realized again that "he is not with us" and the terror of the thought "often for days overcomes me".

As time wore on, Mary began to find small ways to alleviate her grief. She took to visiting the military hospitals in Washington, distributing food and flowers to the wounded soldiers. She also developed a deep compassion, thanks to her own suffering and her friendship for Lizzie Keckley, for all of the "oppressed colored people". She helped Lizzie to care for "contraband" blacks who were now streaming into Washington and even convinced President Lincoln to donate $200 to her cause because "humanity requires it". Mary also did everything that she could to find jobs for the refugees.

All of this did only so much to ease her pain though and Mary remained unstable. Her mood swings, headaches and explosive temper were worse than ever. In addition, she began to see political conspiracies against her husband everywhere, especially on the part of William Seward, the "dirty sneak" who had tried, and was still trying, to take her husband's job. She despised the man and hated him even more for the fact that he cheerfully ignored her hatred for him.

She believed that all of the Cabinet members were evil and was bothered by the fact that her husband seemed to be so unaware of it. She talked about his enemies in the salon, where the employees passed on her remarks, and sometimes betrayed his confidences --- but only because she wanted to help him. Mary also fretted about his safety, begging Lincoln to take guards along when he went out on his nocturnal walks to the War Department. She begged him to be careful and worried about him so much that it seemed to Lizzie that Mary "read impending danger in every rustling leaf, in every whisper of the wind."

Perhaps the only thing that really provided Mary with any comfort at all was her embrace of Spiritualism, a movement that claimed contact with the dead and which had enjoyed a revival during the years of carnage during the Civil War. Mary began meeting with a number of different Spiritualist mediums and invited many to the White House, as each claimed to be able to "lift the thin veil" and allow Mary to communicate with Willie. Mary's closest spiritualist companion, and one of whom there is some record that Lincoln also met with, was Nettie Colburn Maynard. Many are familiar with a tale told about a séance attended by Nettie Maynard in 1863 where a grand piano levitated. A medium was playing the instrument when it began to rise off the floor. Lincoln and Colonel Simon Kase were both present and it is said that both men climbed onto the piano, only to have it jump and shake so hard that they climbed down. It is recorded that Lincoln would later refer to the levitation as proof of an "invisible power."

Rumors spread that Lincoln had an interest in the spirit world. In England, a piece of sheet music was published which portrayed him holding a candle while violins and tambourines flew about his head. The piece of music was called "The Dark Séance Polka" and the caption below the illustration of the president read "Abraham Lincoln and the Spiritualists".

It was also rumored that Lincoln consulted with these mediums and clairvoyants to obtain information about future events in the war. He found that sometimes they gave him information about matters as mundane as Confederate troop movements --- information that sometimes matched his own precognitive visions. There is much written about Lincoln and the Washington Spiritualists of the day in the accounts and diaries written by friends and acquaintances. One such acquaintance would even claim that Lincoln's plans for the Emancipation Proclamation, which freed the southern slaves, came to him from the spirit of Daniel Webster and other abolitionists of the spirit world.

However, much of the information about Lincoln and his interest in Spiritualism came from the aforementioned Nettie Colburn Maynard, who published a manuscript on the subject in 1891. In the 1850's, a teenaged Nettie became aware of her mediumistic abilities when she discovered that she could induce spirit rappings, or knocking sounds purported to be communications from the other side. Her ability manifested itself during the 1856 James Buchanan and John C. Fremont presidential election, in which Nettie's father, a staunch Fremont supporter, found out how accurate his daughter's talents could be. Too young and inexperienced to comprehend the political differences between the two candidates, she was nevertheless "seized by a power that I could not control" on the day before the election. Grabbing a piece of paper, Nettie scrawled the word "Buchanan" on it and as she did "loud raps came upon the table". Her startled father asked if this meant that Buchanan would win the election. Nettie said that it did and the next day, her prediction proved to be accurate. Her father became convinced that she could help others with her talents.

With her father's approval and support, Nettie went on to become a "spirit lecturer", mainly in New England towns and villages. When the Civil War began in April 1861, despite Northern boasts of a quick victory, she predicted otherwise. "Our spirit friends," she said, "reply ... it would continue four years and require five practically to end it."

Nettie moved to Washington during the years of the war and took up residence in the home of a friend, Mrs. Anna Crosby, whose father had been Robert Mills, the architect who had designed the capitol building. While living in the Crosby home, Nettie met a number of prominent people, including General Simon Cameron and Joshua Speed, one of Lincoln's closest friends. She gave private and public séances for many of these people, and through Spiritualist circles, became acquainted with Mary Lincoln.

According to Nettie, she first met Lincoln on February 5, 1863, during a séance in Georgetown that he was not scheduled to attend. The medium would later claim that her "spirit guide" told her that Lincoln would be in attendance. The host of the party declared that this would never happen, as Lincoln never attended séances away from the White House. To his surprise though, the President did come and the host exclaimed upon seeing him that he had been expected. Lincoln was reportedly shocked and stated that he had not been planning to come but only accompanied Mary on a whim.

During the séance, Lincoln was allegedly contacted by an "old Dr. Bramford", who is said to have given him information about the state of the war. Nettie later quoted the spirit as saying that "a very precarious state of things existed at the front, where General Hooker had just taken command. The army was totally demoralized; regiments stacking arms, refusing to obey orders and do duty; threatening a general retreat; declaring their purpose to return to Washington." She wrote that the vivid picture of this terrible state of affairs seemed to surprise everyone but Lincoln, who spoke up to the spirit. "You seem to understand the situation," he said. "Can you point out the remedy?"

Dr. Bramford replied that he had one, but only if Lincoln had the courage to use it. The President smiled and challenged the eerie voice that was coming to him from the darkness. According to the spirit, the remedy for success lay with Lincoln himself. He spoke: "Go in person to the front; taking with you your wife and children; leaving behind your official dignity, and all manner of display. Resist the importunities of officials to accompany you and take only such attendants as may be absolutely necessary; avoid the high grade officers, and seek the tents of the private soldiers. Inquire into their grievances; show yourself to be what you are. 'The Father of Your People' Make them feel you are interested in their sufferings, and that you are not unmindful of the many trials which beset them in their march through the dismal swamps, whereby both their courage and numbers have been depleted."

Lincoln is said to have replied that if this would do the soldiers good, that such a thing was easily done. The mysterious voice explained that it would do all that was required to unite the soldiers again. In April, Lincoln paid the Army of the Potomac a lengthy visit, arriving at Aquia Creek and traveling by train to Falmouth where Hooker's men were camped. From here, Lincoln could see with a spy glass across the Rappahannock to Fredericksburg, where Robert E. Lee's Army of Virginia waited, less than a half mile away. A short time later, the over-confident Hooker led the Union to one of the costliest defeats of the war so far at Chancellorsville. No matter what happened in the end though, his men followed him bravely into battle. Had their courage been restored by the visit from President Lincoln?

Nettie Maynard later recalled that after the advice given by Dr. Bramford, the spirit and the President continued to speak about the state of affairs in regards to the war. The spirit also told him that "he would be re-nominated and re-elected to the Presidency." Lincoln was said to have sadly smiled when this was told to him and said, "It is hardly an honor to be coveted, save one could find it his duty to accept it."

It was during this very séance that the famous incident with the levitating piano took place. The medium said to have performed this wonder was Mrs. Belle Miller, a prominent Washington Spiritualist. Mrs. Miller was playing the piano and under her influence, it "rose and fell", keeping time to her touch in a regular manner. One of those present suggested that, as an added test of the invisible power causing the instrument to move, Belle placed her hand on the piano, standing at an arm's length from it, to show that she was in no way connected to it except as an agent. President Lincoln then placed his hand underneath the piano, at the end nearest Mrs. Miller, who placed her hand upon his to demonstrate that neither strength nor pressure was being used. In this position, the piano rose and fell a number of times, seemingly at their bidding. Lincoln even changed places to stand on the other side of the piano, but the same thing continued to happen.

The President was reported to have grinned at the display and said that he believed he could hold the instrument to the floor. He climbed up onto it, sitting with his long legs dangling over the side, as did a Mr. Somes, Colonel Simon Kase and a Major in the uniform of the Federal Army. The piano, ignoring the enormous weight now upon it, continued to wobble up and down until the sitters were obliged to "vacate the premises".

The audience was, by this time, satisfied to the fact that no mechanical means had been used to move the instrument and Lincoln himself declared that he was sure the motion was caused by some "invisible power".

"Mr. President, " said Mr. Somes, "when I have related to my acquaintances that which I have experienced tonight, they will say, with a knowing look and a wise demeanor, 'you were psychologized and as a matter of fact, you did not see what you in reality did see."

"You should bring that person here," Lincoln quietly replied, "and when the piano seems to rise, have him slip his foot under the leg and be convinced by the weight of the evidence resting upon his understanding."

His sly comment brought a wave of laughter to the room but when the chuckles died down, the President wearily sank into an armchair, "the old, tired, anxious look returning to his face."

Nettie Maynard held a number of séances with Mary and Lincoln during the latter months of February and early March 1863, not long after Willie's death. The séances all took place by appointment and after the close of the session, Mary would make another appointment to come at a certain hour of another day, usually around the time that the President took his lunch in the afternoon.

On one occasion, Nettie was summoned to a séance by Mr. Somes, who told her that the meeting was of such a private nature that he was not at liberty to say more. Somes picked her up in a carriage that evening and informed her that her destination was the White House. He explained that while at the War Department that afternoon, he had met President Lincoln coming from Secretary Stanton's office. Somes spoke to him briefly and Lincoln asked him if he knew whether or not Nettie was in the city and if so, would it be possible for her to visit the White House that night. When Somes told her that Nettie was indeed in Washington, Lincoln asked that she come that evening but that the matter should be kept confidential.

By the time that Somes had finished explaining what had occurred, the carriage had arrived at the White House. A waiting servant ushered them inside and they were hurried up to the President's office, where Lincoln and two other men were waiting. The President sent the servant out of the room and a few moments later, Mary entered the chamber. Lincoln told Nettie that he wished for her to give the visitors an opportunity to witness something of her "rare gift" and he added that "you need not be afraid, as these friends have seen something of this before."

Nettie described the men as being military officers, although their coats had been buttoned to conceal any insignia or mark of rank. One of the men was tall and heavily built, with auburn hair and dark eyes. He had thick side whiskers and carried himself like a soldier. The other man was of average height and she had the impression that he was of a lesser rank than his companion. He had light brown hair and blue eyes and was quick in manner but deferential towards his friend.

The group sat quietly for a few moments and then Nettie entered a trance. One hour later, she became conscious of her surroundings and was standing at a table upon which was a large map of the Southern states. She held a lead pencil in her hand and Lincoln and the two men were standing close to her, bending over the map. The younger man was looking curiously and intently at her.

"It is astonishing," Mr. Lincoln was saying to the larger of the soldiers, "how every line she has drawn conforms to the plan agreed upon."

"Yes," answered the other man. "It is astonishing."

Looking up, both of the men saw that she was awake and they instantly stepped back. Lincoln took the pencil from Nettie's hand and eased her into a nearby chair. Mary soon appeared at her side to offer some comfort.

"Was everything satisfactory?" Somes asked the assembled men.

"Perfectly", Lincoln replied. "Miss Nettie does not seem to require eyes to do anything."

Shortly after, the conversation turned to more mundane matters and after a brief time, the military men took their leave and then it came the President's time to depart. He carefully shook Nettie's small hand and said to her in a low voice: "It is best not to mention this meeting at the present."

This was the last time that the private séance was ever mentioned and Nettie never learned the identity of the two men who were with President Lincoln that night --- or just what the spirits may have revealed with the map of the Confederacy.

According to accounts, Nettie Maynard's contact with the next world was said to have brought relief to Lincoln on more than one occasion. She was at the White House to visit Mrs. Lincoln in May 1863, around the time that the battle of Chancellorsville was being fought. Nettie was brought into Mary's bedroom and found the First Lady wearing only her dressing gown. Her hair was loose and she was pacing back and forth in a distracted manner. "Oh Miss Nettie," Mary cried, "such dreadful news; they are fighting at the front; such terrible slaughter; and all our generals are killed and our army is in full retreat; such is the latest news. Oh, I am glad you have come. Will you sit down a few moments and see if you can get anything from the beyond?"

As no news of the battle had yet reached the public, Nettie was surprised by what she heard. She put her things aside and sat down with Mary to let her "spirit guide" take control of her. In a few moments, she was able to reassure Mary that her fears were groundless. A great battle was being fought but the Union forces were holding their own and while many thousands had been killed, none of the generals, as she had been informed, were slain or injured. She would, Nettie assured her, receive better news by nightfall.

This calmed Mary somewhat but when President Lincoln entered the room a short time later, it was obvious that he was still anxiously worrying about what was occurring at the front lines. He greeted Nettie with little enthusiasm but Mary insisted that he listen to what the medium had to say. Lincoln listened attentively to what had been passed on from Nettie's "spirit guide", recounting the true conditions at the front and assuring him of the news that he would receive before nightfall and the following morning. The battle would be costly but not disastrous and though not decisive in any way, it would not be a loss to the Union cause. Lincoln brightened visibly under the assurances that he was given and he later learned that Nettie's information had been correct. Chancellorsville resulted in the lives of many men lost and effectively ended the career of General Joseph Hooker but no real ground was lost by the Union. Hooker had marched into a Confederate controlled area and his outnumbered army was sent into retreat but regrouped to fight another day.

As time and the war marched on, Lincoln came to believe that a portent of doom hung over his head. The constant threats of death and violence that he received kept he and his bodyguards on edge at all times. It is also believed that some of his spiritualist friends felt the end was near.

During the winter of 1864 and 1865 though, the war was nearing its end. In February 1865, Washington was filled to capacity with people who had come to witness the second inauguration of President Lincoln and Nettie received a dispatch from home, informing her that her father had taken ill. She was asked to come home at once. Having an appointment to meet with Mary soon after, she made a trip to the White House to tell her that she had to leave town. Mary was out, so Nettie proceeded upstairs to have a word with the President instead.

It was the early part of the afternoon, and during the last days of the expiring Congress, and the waiting room was filled with members of both Houses, all anxious to get a word with the President. Nettie soon became doubtful that she would obtain any time with Mr. Lincoln, especially in light of the fact that many of the prominent men had been waiting for several hours. Edward, Lincoln's devoted usher, was walking back and forth and collecting calling cards to take into the President and Nettie called him over. She explained that she needed only a brief moment with Lincoln and asked for any opportunity to tell him why she would have to cancel her appointment the following week.

Half an hour went by and Edward appeared and asked Nettie to follow him. Several of the senators that Nettie knew personally laughed to her and asked with a smile that she put in a good word for them. She was soon in the presence of the President. He stood at his desk, looking over some papers but laid them down and greeted her with a genial smile. In as few words as possible, knowing how precious his time was, she informed him of her unusual call and told him that she had been summoned out of town because her father was seriously ill. Lincoln looked at her with a curious smile. "But cannot our friends from the upper country tell you whether his illness is likely to prove fatal or not?"

Nettie replied that she had already consulted with her "friends" and that they had assured her that his treatment was wrong and that her presence was needed to affect a cure.

Lincoln laughed and turned to his secretary. "I didn't catch her, did I?", he teased Nettie and then seriously added that he was sorry that she would be away during the inauguration.

"I would enjoy it," she assured him, "but the crowd will be so great that we will not be able to see you, Mr. Lincoln, even if I remain."

"You could not help it," he answered, drawing his lean figure to its full height and glancing at her in an amused way. " I will be the tallest man there."

"That is true, in every sense of the word."

Lincoln nodded pleasantly at the compliment and then asked Nettie what her "friends" predicted for his future.

"What they predicted for you, Mr. Lincoln, has come to pass and you are to be inaugurated for the second time." He nodded his head and she continued. "But they also reaffirm that the shadow they have spoken of still hangs over you."

Lincoln shook his head impatiently. "Yes, I know," he said quickly. "I have letters from all over the country from your kind of people --- mediums, I mean --- warning me against some dreadful plot against my life. But I don't think the knife is made, or the bullet run, that will reach it. Besides, nobody wants to harm me."

A feeling of sadness overwhelmed Nettie. It was a feeling that she could not account for and also one that she could not conceal. She spoke to the President boldly: "Therein lies your danger, Mr. President --- your overconfidence in your fellow men."

The old melancholy look that Nettie had grown so used to in her time of friendship with the President and his wife descended over his face. His voice was quiet and subdued. "Well, Miss Nettie," he said, "I shall live until my work is done and no earthly power can prevent it. And then it doesn't matter so that I am ready and that I ever mean to be."

Then, brightening a little, he extended his hand to her. "Well. I suppose that I must bid you goodbye but we shall hope to see you back again next fall."

"I shall certainly come," Nettie told him, "if you are still here."

With another cordial shake of the President's hand, Nettie passed out of Lincoln's presence for the last time. "Never again," she later wrote, "would we meet his welcome smile."

7. DREAMS OF DEATH

Perhaps the most famous supernatural incident connected to Lincoln was the much written about prophetic dream that he had on the eve of his assassination. Some believe there were other warnings as well --- or at least curious coincidences that may not have been realized at the time but would be seen as dire foreshadowing's in the years to come. One such eerie happening involved a photograph that many have come to believe was a prophetic warning of a future to come.

The tide of the bloody Civil War finally turned in favor of the Union during the autumn of 1864, just in time to secure the re-election of Abraham Lincoln. His second inauguration took place on March 4, 1865, a stormy morning that had been plagued by rain and chilling winds. A drenching downpour had fallen all morning but when Lincoln took the stage, the rain suddenly stopped and the sun appeared.

During these bright moments, a photograph was taken by the great Civil War photographer Alexander Gardner. To many, this has become known as one of the most chilling photographs in American history. On the finished plate, President Lincoln himself has been completely blotted out by a careless thumbprint that was pressed on the wet negative. However clearly visible are six men who, less than six weeks later, would be implicated in Lincoln's murder. To the left of the photograph, beneath the platform and standing together, are five men. They have been identified as Lewis Payne (or Powell), who tried to stab Secretary of State Seward on the night of Lincoln's death; David Herold, who held Powell's horse and helped him escape; George Atzerodt, who was assigned to kill Vice President Andrew Johnson but lost his nerve; John Surratt, a Confederate spy whose mother owned a boarding house where the conspirators to kill Lincoln met; and Edman Spangler, a laborer at Ford's Theater, who helped the killer to escape.

But to the right of Lincoln, above him and standing near a statue, is John

Wilkes Booth, the man who fired the fatal shot into Lincoln's head. Booth's handsome face stands out in the crowd and his close placement to the President was possible thanks to his engagement to a Senator's daughter. Standing just below Booth was John T. Ford, one of the owners of Ford's Theater.

Booth would later lament: "What an excellent chance that would have been to kill the President". One has to wonder how the tide of history might have changed if Booth had carried out his plans on that day instead of on that "Black Friday" in April.

Lincoln's dream of death has become known as a famous incident but as mentioned, Lincoln was not the only person who experienced a foreshadowing of that dire event. Spiritualists all over the world were deluging the White House offices with letters warning the president of danger.

Of course, it could be said that these letters were not really convincing evidence of paranormal predictions. As the war dragged on, threats of death and murder seemed to multiply. Lincoln's bodyguards, as well as the soldier assigned to his protection, were constantly thwarted from their duty by Lincoln himself. He often slipped out of the White House at night for solitary strolls and refused to take precautions that were necessary to keep him protected. Many felt that it was only a matter of time before the assassin's bullet caught up with the President.

One of Lincoln's old friends from Illinois was a lawyer with whom he had ridden the legal circuit named Ward Hill Lamon. He was the same man who had assisted Lincoln in slipping into Washington before his first inauguration. Lincoln had later appointed him to a security position in the White House and he worried constantly over Lincoln's seeming indifference to threats and warnings of death. Lamon often resigned his position because his friend did not take the danger seriously. Lincoln always convinced him to stay on, promising to be more careful ---- as he vanished out of the White House at night, or attended the theater without protection.

Lamon became obsessed with watching over Lincoln and many believe that the president would not have been killed at Ford's Theater had Lamon been on duty that night. As it turned out, the security chief happened to be in Richmond, Virginia, on an errand for the president, when disaster struck. He would never forgive himself for what happened --- especially since he believed that he had a forewarning of the event, from Lincoln himself.

Years later, Lamon would remember that Lincoln had always been haunted by the strange vision that he experienced in the mirror in 1860. Several years after that, it was to Lamon and Mary Lincoln to whom the president would recount an eerie dream of death, just shortly before his assassination.

"About ten days ago, I retired late. I soon began to dream. There seemed to be a death-like stillness about me. Then I heard subdued sobs, as if a number of people were weeping. I thought I left my bed and wandered downstairs. There the silence was broken by the same pitiful sobbing, but the mourners were invisible. I went from room to room; no living person was in sight, but the same mournful sounds of distress met me as I passed along.

"It was light in all the rooms; every object was familiar to me, but where were all the people who were grieving as if their hearts would break? I was puzzled and alarmed. What could be the meaning of all this? Determined to find the cause of a state of things so mysterious and so shocking, I kept on until I arrived at the East Room, which I entered. Before me was a catafalque, on which rested a corpse wrapped in funeral vestments. Around it were stationed soldiers who were acting as guards; and there was a throng of people, some gazing mournfully upon the corpse, whose face was covered, others weeping pitifully.

" 'Who is dead in the White House?', I demanded of one of the soldiers.

" 'The President', was his answer, 'He was killed by an assassin.'

"Then came a loud burst of grief from the crowd, which awoke me from my dream. I slept no more that night; and although it was only a dream, I have been strangely annoyed by it ever since."

Lincoln was murdered just a few days later and his body was displayed in the East Room of the White House. Mary would recall this dream of her husband's quite vividly in the days that followed. It was said that her first coherent word after the assassination was a muttered statement about his dream being prophetic.

On April 14, 1865, a few days after the horrifying dream and on the night he was to attend Ford's Theater, Lincoln called a meeting of his cabinet. Edwin Stanton, Lincoln's Secretary of War, arrived 20 minutes late and the meeting began without him. As Stanton and Attorney General James Speed were leaving the meeting, Stanton commented to him that he was pleased about how much work was accomplished.

"But you were not here at the beginning", Speed said. "When we entered the council chamber, we found the President seated at the top of the table, with his face buried in his hands. Presently, he raised it and we saw that he looked grave and worn".

"Gentlemen, before long, you will have important news", the President told them. The Cabinet members were anxious to hear what news Lincoln spoke of, but he refused to tell them anything further.

"I have heard nothing, but you will hear tomorrow," he said, and then continued, "I have had a dream. I have dreamed three times before; once before the Battle of Bull Run; once on another occasion; and again last night. I am in a boat, alone on a boundless ocean. I have no oars, no rudder, I am helpless. I drift!"

That evening, while attending a performance of a play called "Our American Cousin" at Ford's Theater, Lincoln was killed by an assassin named John Wilkes Booth. He died the next morning, April 15, the anniversary of the southern assault on Fort Sumter, the event that officially started the Civil War.

Lincoln spoke of death and prophecies to other members of his staff also, like Colonel W.H. Crook, a member of the White House security team and one of Lincoln's personal bodyguards. Crook took his task seriously, often staying awake at night and sitting outside Lincoln's bedroom while the president slept. Crook even refused to read a newspaper while on duty so that he would be ready should an emergency arise.

Crook was on duty the evening of April 14 and that same afternoon, Lincoln spoke to him about the strange dreams that he had been having. Crook pleaded with the President not to go to the theater that night, but Lincoln dismissed his concerns, explaining that he had promised Mary they would go and that he needed a night away from the problems of the country. Crook then asked to accompany the president, but Lincoln again refused, insisting that Crook could not work around the clock.

Lincoln had a habit of bidding Crook a "good night" each evening as he left the office and went to his bedroom. On that fateful day, according to Crook, Lincoln paused as he left for the theater and turned to the bodyguard. "Good-bye, Crook," he said significantly.

"It was the first time that he neglected to say 'Good Night' to me", Crook would later recall. "And it was the only time that he ever said 'Good-bye'. I thought of it at that moment and, a few hours later, when the news flashed over Washington that he had been shot, his last words were so burned into my being that they can never be forgotten."

Lincoln's final premonition was not the last however. General Ulysses S. Grant and his wife Julia were also scheduled to attend the performance of "Our American Cousin" that night. But that morning, Julia awoke with a terrible sensation. She wanted to leave Washington immediately, despite the fact that the entire city was celebrating her husband's victory over Lee and the surrender of the Confederate armies.

She was sure that something terrible was about to happen.

General Grant, who according to the plans of the conspirators was also supposed to be assassinated, was not present at Ford's Theater because Julia simply refused to attend the play that night. She pressed Grant so hard about her premonition that he finally agreed not to go.

Would Grant have also been killed that night if he had attended the performance? Thanks to Julia Grant's strange premonition, we will thankfully never know.

8. SPIRITS OF THE ASSASSINATION

Now he belongs to the ages.....

Edwin M. Stanton, U.S. Secretary of War, at President
Lincoln's deathbed on April 15, 1865

On a cool Sunday evening, April 9, 1865, President Lincoln was returning home from a visit at the bedside of Secretary of State Stanton, who was recuperating from a broken jaw, when a messenger arrived with a telegram from General Grant. The end had come - the Confederate armies had surrendered! The great war had finally ended and now Lincoln could only think of the best ways to repair the ties with the embattled and defeated South. He knew that the radicals in Congress would seek revenge against the Confederate states but for now they were fearful of Lincoln's popularity with the voters. Lincoln knew that when things calmed down that he had to have a policy of mercy solidified for the Union. He had to think carefully and coolly before he spoke to the crowds that formed outside of the White House on Monday evening, demanding a speech. When they stormed so loud outside of the windows that he could not deny them, he appeared for a moment, joking with them, putting them off and pretending to be unprepared. Finally, he slipped out of the situation by setting the band to strike up "Dixie".

The next night, Tuesday, the crowd returned, larger and more insistent than ever. Slowly, the President appeared on the steps, his face saddened by the loss of so many lives over the years. Sagely, he began to express quiet, merciful thoughts to those who crowded onto the White House lawn. He spoke of the joys of peace, saying nothing of punishment for the "rebels". He spoke of God and thanksgiving, not of vengeance. What had to be done was to get the Southerners back into the Union as tactfully as possible. "We all agree," he said, "that the seceded states so called, are out of their proper practical relation with the Union, and that the sold object of the government, civil and military, in regard to those states, is to again get them into that proper relation. I believe that it is not only possible, but in fact easier, to do this without deciding or even considering whether these states have ever been out of the Union, than with it. Finding themselves safely at home, it would be utterly immaterial whether they had ever been abroad."

These were the first words that Lincoln spoke concerning reconciliation with the former Confederacy but they would not be the last. Over the three days that followed, peace and reconciliation "smoothed out the Mason and Dixon line".

Not surprisingly, Lincoln's mood was high and he felt exhilarated to know that the war had finally ended. He saw only good things on the horizon. But it would be Mary who saw a forewarning of doom. Lincoln and Mary were riding through the city on Friday afternoon, taking in the air before they arrived at the theater. She kept watching her husband, noting what now seemed to be his strange animation and unusual joyfulness. Evidently without thinking that he could be elated over the likely triumph of his policy of mercy, she was gripped with a sudden fear: "I have seen you thus only once before," she said, "it was just before our dear Willie died."

At the mention of his son's death, which had staggered him and haunted his dreams, Lincoln lost his cheerfulness and settled back into the same melancholy that had, since his youth, seemed "to drip from him as he walked". After a time though, his spirits lifted somewhat and by evening, when the curtain rose at the theater, he was optimistic once more.

Northerners, wanting life and laughter in the madness of victory, rushed to the theater to celebrate. It was Good Friday, which was usually a terrible night for theater owners, but it was a wondrous one in Washington of 1865. Ford's Theater was especially packed that night for it had been announced that both Lincoln and Grant planned to show themselves in public. Everyone wanted to see the men who had guided the country so mysteriously to overwhelming success.

The theater was full to the doors as the curtain went up and the play began but the audience gave only half its attention to the actors on the stage. They watched the President's empty box and waited for him to arrive.

When the Civil War ended, it did not end for everyone in Washington. There were many, in the north and the south, who refused to believe that the Confederacy had fallen.

One of these men was John Wilkes Booth, an actor who professed and undying devotion to the South. Booth was the son of Junius Brutus Booth, a professional actor. The elder Booth was considered by many to be so eccentric that he was nearly insane, a trait which father and son apparently shared. John Wilkes Booth was also the brother of Edwin Booth, perhaps the most famous stage actor of the period. Edwin often spoke of his brother's strangeness and he would have had an even greater cause for concern had he known the dark secrets that his sibling hid in his heart.

While the war was still raging, Booth had been attempting to organize a paramilitary operation with a small

John Wilkes Booth

group of conspirators. Their plan was to kidnap the president and take him to Richmond. After a number of failed attempts, it was clear that the plan would not work. Booth's hatred of Lincoln forced him to change his plans from kidnapping to murder. He did not explain to his confederates about this change until two hours before the event took place.

Booth had been a southern sympathizer throughout the war. He was revered for his acting in the South and during the war had been a spy and a smuggler, working with southern agents in Maryland and Canada. He was also rabid in his pro-slavery views, believing that slavery was a "gift from God". He was convinced that Lincoln was a tyrant and Booth hoped the murder of the president would plunge the North into chaos and allow the Confederacy to rally and seize control of Washington.

On the night of April 14, Booth stepped into Lincoln's box at Ford's Theater and shot the president in the back of the head. At the same time, another assassin tried to kill Secretary of State Seward. He was horribly scarred by a knife wound to the face, but survived. Secretary of War Edwin Stanton and General Grant were also slated to be killed and presidential successor Andrew Johnson was only spared because of an assassin's cold feet. The shadow of a greater conspiracy hung over Washington and many questions have not been answered to this day, including whether Edwin Stanton was also involved in the assassination.

Some historians (and conspiracy theorists) believe that Stanton was one of the few to really gain by Lincoln's death. There was no question that Stanton had long been standing in Lincoln's shadow, so to speak, and was violently opposed to many of the President's policies. He favored a revenge policy of radical Reconstruction for the Southern states and was enraged over Lincoln's gentle plans for rebuilding the South. Stanton would have gained even more power if the North had imposed a military occupation on the former Confederacy. Many believe that Stanton's behavior both before and after Lincoln's assassination raised many questions about his loyalty. For example:

- Stanton refused a request for Major Thomas Eckert to accompany Lincoln to Ford's Theater. The implication, according to some historians, was that Stanton knew something Lincoln didn't.

- Despite Lincoln's many death threats, Stanton only sent one bodyguard to the theater that night and this man abandoned his post to have a drink. He was never reprimanded for this.

- On the night of the assassination, telegraph lines in Washington, controlled by the War Department, mysteriously went dead, delaying the news of Booth's escape. Many believe this points to some sort of government conspiracy behind the murder.

- Booth's diary was given to Stanton after the assassination and it vanished for several years. When it was returned, eighteen pages were missing. A security chief would later testify that it had been intact when given to Stanton.

And there were other problems as well, although none of this would be brought to light until more than 70 years later! It was, of course, far too late by that time but the mystery remains as to whether or not Stanton was in some way involved. Was Mary Lincoln's hatred and distrust of the man not as displaced as many once believed? We will never know but there is no question that many other mysteries of the Lincoln assassination also remain unsolved.

The Lincoln party arrived at the theater and entered their reserved box, which had been adorned with drapes and Union flags, to the cheers of the crowd and to the musical strains of "Hail to the Chief". On stage, the actors ceased their dialogue in deference to Lincoln The play was a production called "Our American Cousin", presented by actress Laura Keene. The play was a comedy, the sort of show that Lincoln liked best. The Lincoln's were accompanied by a young couple, Major Henry Rathbone and his fiancée, Clara Harris. Lincoln slumped

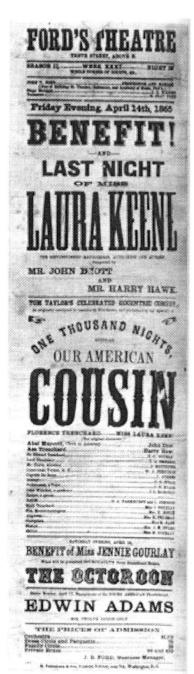

(Left) An advertising for the play attended by the Lincoln's on that fateful night
(Above) The President's box at Ford's Theater
(Illinois State Historical Society)

into a rocking chair that had been provided by the management to fit his long body and Mary was seated beside him, with Rathbone and Clara Harris to their right. On stage, Harry Hawk, the male lead, ad-libbed a line: "This reminds me of a story, as Mr. Lincoln would say". The audience roared and clapped and Lincoln smiled, whispering something to Mary. Behind him, the box door was closed but not locked and in all of the excitement over the President's arrival, no one noticed the small peep hole that had been dug out of it.

As the play progressed, guard John Parker left his post in the hallway outside of the box and either went down into the gallery to watch the play or left to have a drink. Those who believe there was a government conspiracy to kill Lincoln often point to John Parker as proof of it. Parker vas Lincoln's only bodyguard that night and he had gone ahead to Ford's Theater that evening that evening rather than accompany the President to the venue. A patrolman on the Washington police force, Parker was a lazy drunk with an appalling history of insubordination and insufficiency. He was totally unsuitable to guard the President and it is believed that if Ward Hill Lamon had been aware of the posting, he would have never allowed himself to be removed from the detail that night.

On stage, the players hammed it up in silly and melodramatic scenes and laughter rolled through the audience. As the Lincoln's picked up the story, Hawk was a homespun American woodsman named Asa Trenchard and Laura Keene, a stunning actress with thick auburn hair, was his young English cousin, Florence Trenchard. A scheming English matron named Mrs. Mountchessington, convinced that Asa was a rich Yankee, was out to snare him for her daughter Augusta. Lincoln chuckled along with the play, trying to keep his mind off of the troubles that lay ahead. Mary rested her hand on his knee and called his attention to situations on the stage and applauded happily at the funniest scenes. One of the actresses noted that while Lincoln never clapped, he did laugh "heartily" from time to time.

Meanwhile, John Wilkes Booth had been lurking about the theater all evening and finally approached the state box, where the Lincoln's and their guests were seated. He showed a card to an attendant and gained access to the outer door, which he found to be unattended. This should have been completely unexpected but Booth was apparently not surprised by this development. As he slipped into the door of the box, Booth jammed the door closed behind him. The laughter of the crowd concealed any noise that he might have made.

On stage, Mrs. Mountchessington finally discovered the shocking truth about Asa, that he was poor and no catch at all for her daughter. In stiff British rage, she sent Augusta to her room, reproached the American for his ill-mannered impertinence and then marched haughtily into the wings, leaving Asa alone on the stage.

During the evening, the Lincoln party had been discussing the Holy Land. The President made a comment about wanting to visit Jerusalem someday as he leaned forward and noticed General Ambrose Burnside in the audience of the theater. At that moment, Booth stepped forward. Major Rathbone stood from his seat to confront the intruder but before he could act, Booth raised a small pistol and fired it into the back of President Lincoln's head.

Rathbone seized the actor but Booth slashed him with a knife. Lincoln fell forward, striking his head on the rail of the box and slumping over. Mary took hold of him, believing him to have simply fallen while Booth jumped from the edge of the balcony. His boot snagged on the bunting across the front of the box and he landed badly, fracturing his leg. As he struggled to his feet, he cried out

"Sic Semper Tyrannis!" (Thus it shall ever be for tyrants) and he stumbled out of the theater using the back stage door. Both Rathbone and Clara Harris began to cry after him, "Stop that man! Stop that man!"

"Won't somebody stop that man," Clara pleaded. "The President is shot!"

Her final scream snapped the audience out of its stunned stupor. Soon, voices began to take up the call of "Booth!", having recognized the famous actor as he plunged to the stage. In spite of this however, he managed to easily escape from the close and crowded auditorium. Then, there were more screams, groans and the crashing of seats ---- but above it all, came Mary Lincoln's shrill and terror-filled scream for her husband.

Dr. Charles Augustus Leale, the first doctor to reach President Lincoln after he was shot

By now, the theater was in chaos. People were shoving into the aisles and rushing for the exits, with Laura Keene yelling at them from the stage: "For God's sake, have presence of mind and keep your places, and all will be well."

In the theater's audience was a young doctor named Charles Leale, who rushed upstairs to Lincoln's aid. He fought his way into the President's box, where a weeping Clara Harris tried to console Mary, who was holding Lincoln in the rocker and weeping hysterically. Leale lay the President on the floor and removed the blood clot from the wound to relieve the pressure on the brain. The bullet had struck him just behind the left ear, had traveled through the brain and lodged behind his right eye. Even this young doctor could see that the wound was a fatal one --- the President was nearly dead. Lincoln's heart was barely beating but Leale reached into his mouth, opened his throat and applied artificial respiration in a desperate attempt to save him. A few moments later, Leale was joined by Dr. Charles Sabin Taft and the two men continued their efforts. They raised and lowered the President's arms, while Leale massaged his chest, and then he forced his own breath into Lincoln's lungs again and again. At last, he was breathing on his own, his heart beating with an irregular flutter. The President was failing --- but he was still alive.

The two doctors, with some help from bystanders, managed to get the President out of Ford's Theater. Soldiers cleared a path through the crowd outside, where people rushed madly back and forth and milled about in confusion.

A man named Henry Safford, who worked as a clerk at the War Department, beckoned to the doctors and they carried the President across the street into the Petersen house. Lincoln's unconscious form was laid in a small, shabby bedroom at the back of the house. His lanky frame was too long for the bed and they were forced to lay him down at an angle. Clara Harris and Major Rathbone, with his untreated arm bleeding profusely, brought Mary to the house. When she saw Lincoln in the back room, Mary ran to him, falling sobbing to her knees and calling him intimate names. She begged Lincoln to speak to her until finally the doctors led her to the front parlor, where she broke into convulsive weeping.

Help was summoned and soon Lincoln's aides and security men were attempting to try and calm the frenzy around them. Meanwhile, the Surgeon General, Joseph K. Barnes, and Lincoln's own doctor, Robert Stone King, set to work on the President. They soon realized that it was no use --- there was nothing that could be done for him.

By now, word had spread through Washington and a procession of government officials came running to the house, crowding into the room where Lincoln lay with a cluster of doctors at his side. Robert Lincoln arrived with John Hay, barely hearing the words of the doctor who told them at the doorway to the room that it was no use. When he saw his father laying diagonally across the bed, his brain destroyed and his eye swollen and broken with blood, the usually calm and collected young man broke down in despair and disbelief. Finally, in shock himself, he went into the front parlor to try and comfort his mother. Mary had been sedated by one of the doctors though and hardly knew he was there.

As Robert left the room, Senator Charles Sumner entered, his face twisted in anguish. The senator took Lincoln's hand and spoke to him but a doctor assured him that Lincoln was beyond hearing, that he was dead. "No, he isn't dead," Sumner protested in anger. "Look at his face, he is breathing." The other physicians assured him that Lincoln would never regain consciousness and, at that, Sumner clasped Lincoln's hand tightly, bowed his head close to the pillow and began to weep.

With the President near death and the government at a standstill, Secretary of War Stanton took over. Close to breaking down himself, tears burning in his eyes for his beloved friend, Stanton set up headquarters in the back parlor. Here, a Federal judge and two other men helped him to take testimony from the witnesses at the theater. All of them identified the assassin as John Wilkes Booth, the actor and Confederate sympathizer. At the same time, word came that another assassin had attempted but failed to murder Seward and that Washington was being terrorized. At once, Stanton placed the city under martial law and ordered search parties to track down Booth and all other suspects.

As Stanton came and went, issuing orders, calling for Andrew Johnson and mobilizing troops and police officers, Mary lay on the sofa in the front parlor, going back and forth between eerie quiet and fits of weeping. When she recalled Lincoln's dreams of mournful voices in the White House, she cried miserably that his dream had been prophetic. She begged God to take her too or to trade her life for her husband's. Outside the windows of the Petersen house, a crowd gathered in the foggy night, keeping a constant vigil and asking the officials who came and went if there was any word ---- or any hope.

It continued in this way throughout the night. The hours slowly passed and the doctors released half-hourly press bulletins that went out over the telegraph lines about the President's condition. By dawn, the President's condition had worsened and as the first gray light began to appear at the windows, a heavy rain began to fall, as if the heavens were weeping. Sumner was still holding Lincoln's hand when Mary came to see him one last time. She kissed his face and whispered to him, "Love, live but one moment to speak to me once" but then she looked at his shattered face and realized, perhaps for the first time, that he was beyond hope. She wailed as she was led away.

With the end close now, Lincoln's friends and colleagues gathered at his bedside. Stanton and Robert came in from the front room and Robert, giving away to his agony, put his head on Sumner's shoulder. At that, many of the others present also began to cry. Finally, Lincoln took one great breath, his face relaxed and then he faded into oblivion.

The Surgeon General carefully crossed the lifeless hands of Abraham Lincoln at twenty-two minutes after seven on the morning of April 15, 1865.

Edwin Stanton stood by the bedside of the slain president. He raised his head and with tears streaming down his face, uttered the most unforgettable words that a man not known for his poetic soul could ever manage... "Now, he belongs to the ages."

THE MYSTERY OF JOHN WILKES BOOTH

After shooting the President, John Wilkes Booth escaped from Washington on horseback across the Anacostia Bridge, passing a sentry who had not yet learned of the assassination. He made it to a farm in Virginia with the help of his fellow conspirators, only stopping to rest because of the leg that he broke when he jumped from the President's theater box.

Soon, the hunt for Lincoln's assassin was on and by morning, more than 2,000 soldiers were looking for Booth. On April 26, a detachment of 25 men finally tracked down Booth, and a comrade named David Herold, at a tobacco farm near Port Royal, Virginia. The barn where they were hiding was surrounded and Herold decided to surrender. He was manacled and tied to a tree. Booth decided to die rather than be taken alive --- or so the history books say.

In the darkness outside, a decision was made to try and smoke Booth out. The barn was set on fire and in a few moments, the interior was engulfed in flames. Booth came to the door and raised his weapon, apparently looking for a target among the soldiers outside. One of the soldiers, a Sergeant Boston Corbett, saw Booth through the slats of the barn and, ignoring Edwin Stanton's specific orders to bring Booth back alive, shot him in the back of the head. Booth fell to the floor and the soldiers rushed to subdue him. He died two hours later, whispering instructions to tell his mother that he "died for his country and did what he thought best."

A search of the dead man's pockets turned up a few items, including a compass; a diary; and photographs of several women, along with one portrait of Booth's fiancée, Lucy Hale.

Booth died on the porch of the farm house as light was beginning to show in the sky. The dead man was sewn into a burlap bag and was taken to Alexandria on a steamer. Booth's body was then placed on a carpenter's bench and identified from a crude tattoo of the actor's initials; by dental fillings; and by a scar on the back of his neck. Others claimed that the body only resembled Booth, but that it actually wasn't him at all. Regardless, the corpse was taken to the Old Penitentiary in Washington and, using a gun case for a coffin, was buried under the floor of the old dining room. The door to the room was locked and the body stayed there for another four years. Finally, pleas from Edwin Booth convinced President Andrew Johnson to allow the body to be exhumed and buried in an unmarked grave in the family plot in Baltimore.

But was it really the body of John Wilkes Booth in the grave?

The man who shot Booth, Sergeant Boston Corbett, had been assigned to Lieutenant Edward Doherty and had been given the task of helping to track down the assassin. The soldiers found several witnesses who recognized Booth and eventually discovered sympathizer Willie Jett, who had arranged lodging for Booth at the tobacco farm where he was later discovered.

It was Corbett who fired the fatal bullet that killed Booth. It was at this point where many of the conspiracy theories begin. Among the theories is the idea that Corbett was under different orders than the other soldiers. Some believe he was actually told to silence Booth so that William Seward could not be implicated in the plot. It is unlikely that this was the case however, as Corbett is not believed to have had contact with Seward before leaving Washington. He did act on orders to kill Booth however, if not orders from Seward, then from a higher authority.

He shot Booth on direct orders from God.

Corbett was a religious fanatic who believed that he was directed by voices from heaven. This is ironic considering that Booth also claimed to be acting on orders from God when he killed President Lincoln.

Corbett had been in the hat-making industry prior to the war and had been exposed to large quantities of mercury, which often caused insanity in this trade (thus, the expression "mad as a hatter"). Although he fought bravely in the Federal Army, his odd and erratic behavior often made his superiors wary about using him in some assignments. As a radical fundamentalist Christian, Corbett also reportedly castrated himself in 1858 after being solicited by a prostitute. Needless to say, this ended his temptation for fleshly sins. He also refused any alcohol and often condemned his fellow soldiers who drank.

Could Seward, or some other conspirator in the government, have used this unbalanced man as a pawn in the assassination plot? Perhaps, for he certainly would have followed any orders presented in a way that made him believe he was involved in some holy crusade.

After the war, Corbett moved to Kansas, where he became the security chief for the state legislature. He stayed in this position until one day when he pulled a gun on two boys who were mocking a minister's sermon. After that, he was committed to the Topeka Asylum for the Insane. However, in 1888, Corbett escaped and seemingly vanished from the pages of history.

But the man who Corbett allegedly killed, while surely the murderer of Abraham Lincoln, didn't fade away quite so easily.

The newspapers quickly spread the word that President Lincoln's assassin, gunned down in a Virginia barn, was the actor John Wilkes Booth. There is no doubt in anyone's mind that the killer had been Booth, but the question remains as to whether or not Booth himself was ever brought to justice. That question still remains unanswered today.

Shortly after the assassin was gunned down, the word began to spread that it might not have been Booth in that barn after all. The government's handling of the body in question and of the witnesses who were present, did not add much credence to the official version of the story. The Union soldiers had certainly killed a man. The War Department and the newspapers told a breathless nation that the man had been John Wilkes Booth --- but had it really?

From the day the body was brought back to Washington, there were already people on the streets denying the body was that of Booth. They believed the assassin had long since escaped and that the government was offering a secret substitution for the real killer.

The War Department took a firm position on the matter and would not argue it further. They maintained that the corpse was Booth. In their possession were items that belonged to him and other evidence that proved they had the right man, including the left boot that Booth had abandoned to put his broken leg in splints; the revolver he had been carrying when killed; and affidavits from the soldiers who brought the body back, claiming that the face of the corpse matched the photos of Booth they had been given. The investigators studied these, but they were never shown to the public. The government refused to even consider the idea that the body might not be that of Booth.

In the official silence from Washington, people began to see something dark and mysterious. They believed there was something strange about the attitude of the government towards Lincoln's murder and towards the killer. Perhaps those who believed in Booth's escape were right in their questioning. They were certainly correct in the knowledge that no one but government employees ever identified the body. It had been quickly hidden away with only certain people allowed to see it. There was not a single witness who was completely impartial, or free from suspicion, who could swear that he had looked at the face of the corpse and that the man had been John Wilkes Booth.

The mystery continued for many years. More than 20 men would later claim to be Booth with books, anecdotes and sworn testimony. The newspapers got hold of each story and fanned the flames of doubt. By June 1865, stories spread that witnesses had seen Booth on a steamer to Mexico, or to South America. It was said that several people saw him in the West and others recognized him in the Orient. In Ohio, a man claimed that Booth had stopped in his tavern on the way to Canada. In the Southwest, several people who claimed to know Booth, said that he owed his escape to Union troopers because of his membership in a fraternal order. They had spirited him away rather than see him hanged. It was no wonder that before long, dark-haired, pallid men who walked with a limp began to be pointed out all across the country as John Wilkes Booth.

The story became so popular that in July 1867, Dr. John Frederick May, who had identified the body as Booth, felt that it was now necessary to make an emphatic denial of his once positive identification. He now stated that he could have been wrong when he said the dead man had been John Wilkes Booth. It seems that two years before the assassination, May had removed a tumor from the back of Booth's neck. The surgery had left a jagged scar behind and this scar was how the doctor had identified the remains. He had been summoned to search for the mark of his scalpel on the corpse that he was supposed to identify.

"The cover was removed from the body", said May, telling of his experience, "and to my great astonishment revealed a body in whose lineaments there was to me no resemblance to the man I had known in life. My surprise was so great that I at once said to General Barnes (the U.S. Surgeon General that Stanton had sent to the inquest)'There is no resemblance to Booth, nor can I believe it to be that of him'. After looking at it a few moments I asked 'Is there a scar upon the back of his neck?'

"He replied, 'There is!'

"I then said, 'If that is the body of Booth, let me describe the scar before it is seen by man', and did so as to its position, its size and general appearance so accurately as to cause him to say, 'You have described the scar as well as if you were looking at it'. The body then being turned, the back of the neck was examined and my mark was unmistakably on it. And it being afterwards, at my request, placed in a sitting position and looking down upon it, I was finally enabled to imperfectly recognize the features of Booth. But never in a human being had a greater change taken place from the man in whom I had seen the vigor and health of life to that of the haggard corpse before me."

This description by the surgeon failed to convince anyone that the body had really been Booth, especially as he continued, bringing to light a more damning bit of evidence. He explained in detail his examination of the corpse in question and its broken right leg. Now, the word of the government, and the witnesses at Ford Theater, said that Booth had broken his left leg when he jumped from the theater box. The fact that the doctor noted that the mysterious body had a broken right leg meant one of two things --- either the body was not Booth's or that Dr. May was too careless of an observer to be credited with any authority in the matter of an accurate identification.

Suspicion thrived across the country and by 1869, President Johnson decided to dispel of all the rumors and allow the assassin's brother to bury the disputed corpse in his family's cemetery plot. On February 15, 1869, government workers exhumed the body that had been buried beneath the floor of the old prison dining hall.

Many believed the mystery of the body would be settled once and for all by Edwin Booth, but he simply added to the confusion by bungling the whole thing. First, he attempted to keep the exhumation a secret and then decided that he couldn't bear to look upon the face of his dead brother. He remained outside of the undertaker's room while friends went inside to examine the corpse. Not surprisingly, they decided the body belonged to John Wilkes Booth.

Needless to say, the public had a good mystery and they weren't about to let it go. A reporter for the Baltimore Gazette was soon claiming that he had been present at the exhumation and that the body had a broken right leg and no bullet holes in it. Modern historians believe this reporter had either a vivid imagination or lied about being at the exhumation at all. Still in those days, the story looked like new evidence that Booth was still alive.

The mystery continued into the 20th century and while Booth's skull was supposedly on display in a number of different traveling carnivals, there remained a question as to his eventual fate. Historians looked for answers in the early 1900's as many of the people involved in the case were still living. Statements were taken from surviving soldiers who aided in Booth's capture and all information was thoroughly researched. They even checked out the claims of men still posing as Booth and found all of them transparently fraudulent.

Could Booth have survived the days after the assassination? The question nagged at historians, although logic would say that he had been killed. Still though, it is interesting that after all of the conflicting evidence, there was not a single eye-witness, sufficiently impartial to be above suspicion, who had seen the corpse in 1865 and could say, with certainty, that it was John Wilkes Booth.

As mentioned, almost every single claim that Booth was alive was quickly exposed as a hoax; however, there were a few of them that weren't and perhaps the most intriguing of these was the case of a man named David E. George, who died in Oklahoma in 1903.

Author W.C. Jameson explains that in order to understand the case of David George, the reader must also understand the history of Finis L. Bates, a young lawyer from Granbury, Texas. Bates was struggling to earn a living in the early 1870's and must have been happy when a man who called himself John St. Helen strolled into his office one day and asked the attorney to defend him against a charge of operating a saloon without a license in the nearby town of Glen Rose. He admitted that he was guilty of the charge but that he did not want to appear in federal court over it. John St. Helen was not his real name, he confessed, and he feared that his identity might be exposed in court.

Bates soon became the man's lawyer and got to know him quite well. He stated that St. Helen seemed to have more money than his status should have allowed and that he had an intimate knowledge of the theater and of the works of Shakespeare, most of which he could recite from memory.

Then, late one night in 1877, Bates was summoned to the sickbed of his client. He was seriously ill and he told Bates that he did not expect to live much longer. He told Bates to reach under his pillow and the attorney took out an old tintype that showed a much younger St. Helen. The sick man told the attorney that if he died, he was to send the photograph to an Edwin Booth in Baltimore with a note that said the subject of the tintype had passed away. In between coughing fits, St. Helen explained to the stunned attorney that his name was actually John Wilkes Booth and that he had assassinated former President Abraham Lincoln.

Bates was shocked and dismayed at the revelation but he knew that he could not betray his client's confidence. He replied that he would send the photograph if needed and he sat next to St. Helen's bed throughout the rest of the night. We could only wonder what thoughts must have been churning in the young man's mind.

However, St. Helen did not die. He remained sick for several weeks but eventually began to recover. Once he was mobile again, he met with Bates and again confessed to being John Wilkes Booth. He begged for the attorney to keep the secret and Bates had no ethical choice but to agree. He did demand some answers though, knowing full well that John Wilkes Booth was reportedly dead.

Booth explained that Andrew Johnson, the vice president, was the principle conspirator behind the assassination. (Interestingly, many theorists agree with this and a number of scenarios exist to explain Johnson's motives as well as Seward's) St. Helen said that he had met with Johnson just hours before Lincoln was killed and Johnson told him that with General Grant away from Washington, Booth would have an easy escape route into Maryland. St. Helen then went on to provide details of the assassination plot, the actual event, his escape from Ford's Theater and flight into the countryside. His descriptions were detailed and to Bates, who initially believed none of the far-fetched story, seemed to have intricacies that only someone intimately involved with the assassination plot would have known. Most of all, they were different enough from the already published accounts of the events that Bates began to give some credibility to St. Helen's version of the story.

St. Helen told the attorney that he had escaped into Kentucky in late April and eventually made his way west of the Mississippi and into the Indian Territory. After spending some time here, he disguised himself as a priest and entered Mexico. In 1867, he traveled to California and met with his mother and older brother Junius in San Francisco. Later, he drifted to New Orleans, where he taught school, and then moved to Texas. Here, he assumed the name John St. Helen and opened a tavern.

He was, he insisted, the assassin known as John Wilkes Booth and Bates humored the man with friendly skepticism and eventually the two men parted ways. Several months after St. Helen's confession, Bates moved to Memphis and established what became a very successful law practice. As the years passed, he developed a deep interest in Abraham Lincoln, especially in the events surrounding his death. In his spare time, he read everything that he could get his hands on about Lincoln and Booth --- and the more he studied, the more convinced that he became that his old client was indeed telling the truth.

John St. Helen, he realized, really had been John Wilkes Booth!

The story of John Wilkes Booth and Finis Bates took another turn in January 1903. On the 13th of that month, the corpse of a man named David E. George arrived at the undertaking parlor of W.B. Penniman in Enid, Oklahoma. George, who had been working in Enid as a handyman and house painter, had apparently committed suicide by ingesting a large dose of strychnine. He was already known as a heavy drinker and was thought to have been depressed of late.

As Penniman's assistant, W.H. Ryan, was embalming George's body, the Reverend E.C. Harper stopped in to the funeral parlor. Harper went into the embalming room and surprised to see the body there, asked Ryan if he knew who the man was? He explained that the dead man was none other than John

Wilkes Booth and that he had confessed his identity to the minister's wife in 1900. Mrs. Harper was summoned and she identified the corpse of David E. George as the man who had told her that he was Booth. She later wrote out and signed a statement, swearing that the confession had taken place.

Over the course of the next few days, a number of newspapers carried the story that a man believed to be Booth had died in Oklahoma. One of the newspaper stories caught the attention of Finis Bates in Memphis and he wondered if the late David E. George might be the man that he had once known as John St. Helen. Curious, he decided to go to Enid and see.

Bates arrived in Oklahoma on January 23 and the next morning, went to the undertaker's to compare the face of the dead man with the tintype photograph that he still possessed. He placed it next to the face of the corpse and compared them. It was, Bates stated without a doubt, the same man!

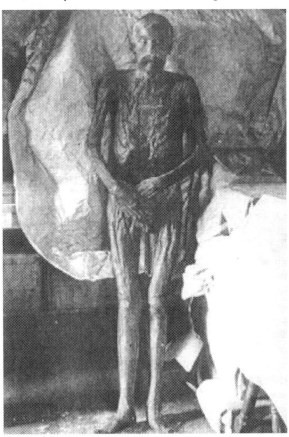

The body remained on display at Penniman's parlor and after it went unclaimed for some time, it was eventually moved into a back room and stored for several years. Eventually, Bates purchased the body and he kept it for many years. In October 1931 though, the mummy was examined by a group of seven doctors at Chicago's Northwestern University. It was studied, x-rayed and dissected and the team did find evidence of a broken leg, although the report did not state whether it was the right or the left. The most compelling discovery was that of a ring that had

The Booth / George Mummy in the 1930's
(E.H. Swain Collection, Georgetown University Library)

somehow become embedded in the flesh of the body cavity. Digestive juices had damaged it over time, but the researchers present believed that the initials

"JWB" could be discerned on the surface of it. Dr. Otto L. Schmidt, who was present and who was the president of the Chicago Historical Society at that time, subsequently wrote "I can say safely that we believe Booth's body is here in my office."

The fate of this intriguing mummy remains a mystery. At one point, Bates tried to sell it to the *Dearborn Independent* for $10,000 and at another time, offered it to Henry Ford for $100,000 but it was declined both times. During the 1920's and 1930's, Bates leased the mummy to a carnival promoter who charged 25-cents to view "The Assassin of President Abraham Lincoln". The mummy was still being displayed into the 1940's but after the promoter went bankrupt and moved to Idaho, he placed the mummy in a chair on his front porch and charged visitors a dime to look at it. Eventually, the mummy disappeared and to this day, no one knows what became of it. It is rumored to be in a private collection somewhere but no one knows for sure.

The final resting place of the mummy is just as mysterious as the questions that linger about John Wilkes Booth. Was Booth and St. Helen / George the same man? Although many feel that Bates tried too hard to make Booth and St. Helen appear to be the same, it can't be ignored that they possessed many of the same characteristics, including heavy drinking, an intimate knowledge of Shakespeare, a penchant for the theater, the same style of dress and the fact that the men were well-educated. In addition, studies of physical characteristics between George and Booth showed many striking similarities, including the shape of their heads, jaw lines and the bridges of both men's noses. And while this doesn't really prove anything, it does make the reader wonder.

There are many problems with the theory, as well. Skeptics states that the color of George's eyes were enough to debunk his claims. His eyes, according to the undertaker, were blue-gray, while government documents say Booth's were black. On the other hand, Asia Booth, the actor's sister, wrote that they were hazel. They also say that Bates wrote that George had a broken right leg, not the left leg that Booth broke jumping from the theater box. Of course, the government's own records stated that the body that was dug up from beneath the floor of the Old Penitentiary had a broken right leg, as well. So, which records were accurate and which were not?

Bates showed photographs of St. Helen and George to a number of people who had known Booth, including those who had seen him perform many times. All of them stated that the man in both photos was John Wilkes Booth.

Another mysterious piece of evidence involved the signet ring worn by Booth. The actor was seldom seen without the ring, which was inscribed with his initials, and he was photographed wearing it many times. The ring was not on the finger of the man who was killed in Virginia. David E. George wore a similar ring, many recalled. Some weeks before his death, George told one of his neighbors that he was being followed. One afternoon, when he saw two sheriffs deputies coming his way, George was so afraid that he would be identified that he removed the ring from his finger and swallowed it. This strange anecdote would provide startling evidence to researchers in 1931 that the body they were examining (with a ring inside of the body cavity!) was that of John Wilkes Booth.

But was it? Who knows? The evidence for the man from Oklahoma being John Wilkes Booth is certainly plausible but unfortunately, so much time has passed, and so much evidence lost, that the answers will likely never be known.

While the question of Booth's capture remains unsolved --- there is suggestion that he does still walk the earth, along with many of the other spirits of the Lincoln assassination. One of the places where Booth's spirit is alleged to walk is Ford's Theater, where the assassin carried out his dark deed.

Shortly after the Lincoln assassination, Ford's Theater was closed down, but it was far from empty. The famous photographer, Matthew Brady, took a picture of the interior of the building. It revealed a nearly transparent figure standing in Lincoln's box. Although not clear, some have suggested that it might be that of John Wilkes Booth.

After the theater was shuttered, John Ford hoped to open it again once the memory of Lincoln's death faded with the public. The citizens of Washington refused to return however and Ford eventually sold the place. It soon became a clearing house for processing Army records. In June 1893, the third floor of the building collapsed and killed a number of staff members.

Finally, in 1933, the theater was given to the National Park Service but its restoration was not begun until 1964. Four years later, it had been turned into a showplace and theatrical museum in the daytime hours and a playhouse at night.

It has been reported that a number of actors, including Hal Holbrook who performed there in his Mark Twain one-man show, have experienced an icy cold presence that can be felt at left center stage. Many forget their lines and tremble involuntarily in the same spot. Some believe the effect is caused by impressions left behind by Booth on the night of the assassination. It has also been reported that mysterious footsteps, weird voices, laughing and the sound of someone weeping can be heard in the darkened theater. Lights have often been known to turn on and off by themselves.

In recent years, a well-known singer was performing at Ford's Theater and complained of being distracted by a light which kept flashing off and on in the restored Lincoln box. The strange thing is that this box is permanently closed to the public, so there could not have been anyone in there. One has to wonder just what she was seeing?

The tragic events of that Good Friday evening in 1865 sparked another chain of events involving people closely embroiled in the assassination. Because when Booth jumped from the theater box that night, he left behind not only a dead president, but several shattered lives as well --- all of them destined to meet tragic ends.

THE CURSE OF MARY LINCOLN

Mary Lincoln, whose mental state had already been declining since the death of Willie in 1862, never recovered from the loss of her husband. She struggled with family problems and more heartbreak and eventually was committed to a mental institution for a time.

Her curse would be that she managed to live 17 years after the death of her husband. For months after his murder, Mary spoke of nothing but the assassination until her friends began to drift away, their sympathy at a breaking point. She began to accuse her husband's friends and his Cabinet members of complicity in the murder, from his bodyguards to Andrew Johnson.

Mary lay in her bed for 40 days after the assassination and in the years that followed, she deteriorated mentally and physically into a bitter old woman who wore nothing but black mourning clothing for the rest of her life. Her attachment to Spiritualism turned into a dangerous obsession, reaching a point where she could not function without aid from her "spirit guides".

Mary also had a great fear of poverty. She often begged her friends to help her with money. Unlike the widows of generals and governors, for whom money was easily raised, Mary's handful of supporters found it impossible to raise funds on her behalf because she was just too unpopular. In fact, she was despised all across America. Newspapers wrote unflattering stories about her and she was ridiculed by members of Washington society.

In 1868, she abandoned America and took Tad to live in Germany. They lived there in hiding for three years before coming home. A government pension awaited her, as did an inheritance from Lincoln's estate, so she was finally a wealthy woman. The ocean crossing had dire circumstances for Tad, however. He developed tuberculosis and although he lingered for six weeks, he eventually passed away.

Mary embraced Spiritualism once again and moved into a commune where she began to develop her psychic "gifts" which enabled her to see "spirit faces" and "communicate beyond the veil". She claimed to have daily conversations with her late husband.

In the Spring of 1875, Robert Lincoln decided to have his mother institutionalized. He was concerned not only for her sanity, but for her estate as well, which he claimed her medium "friends" had designs on. By this time, Robert was wealthy in his own right and had no plans for his mother's money, which Mary refused to understand. He did however hire detectives to follow his mother and gather information about her drug use, which included opium, and he paid doctors to testify about her sanity in court.

Mary was sent to a mental hospital but was later released. She severed all ties with Robert, calling him a "wicked monster". She would hate him for the rest of her days and before she died, she wrote him letters that cursed him and claimed that his father had never really loved him.

Mary went into exile again and moved into a small hotel in France. Her eyes were weakened and her body was wracked with pain from severe arthritis. She refused to travel until several bad falls left her nearly unable to walk. Her sister pleaded with her to come home and finally she returned to Springfield, moving into the same house where she and Lincoln had been married years before.

Mary Lincoln had this photo taken by famed "spirit photographer" William Mumler, claiming that no one else was present at the time of the photo and that the "spirit" of her husband was real. Robert Lincoln believed it to be one more piece of evidence as to his mother's mental instability.

Mary lived the last years of her life in a single room, wearing a money belt to protect her fortune. She kept all of the shades in her room drawn and spent her days packing and unpacking her 64 crates of clothing. She died on July 12, 1882 - a faded shell of the exuberant young socialite that she had once been.

THE "LINCOLN CURSE"

The President's oldest son, Robert, was also no stranger to death and foreboding. He was the only Lincoln son to survive into adulthood and by the time he died in 1926, he was a very haunted man. He believed wholeheartedly that a curse hung over his life.

His strange belief began in 1865 when he was with his father at the time of his death. Needless to say, it was an event that he would never forget.

Sixteen years later, in 1881, Robert was in the company of another American president whose life was ended by an assassin. President James Garfield, who had only been in office about four months, was walking through the railroad station in Washington, accompanied by Robert. Suddenly, a crazed killer named Charles Guiteau appeared from nowhere and gunned down the President.

In 1901, President William McKinley invited Robert Lincoln to tour the Pan-American Exposition with him in Buffalo, New York. While the two men were together, an anarchist named Leon Czolgosg managed to approach them with a pistol. In seconds, President McKinley was dead.

For the third time, Robert had been present at the death of an American president.

Robert Lincoln

Not surprisingly, he became convinced that he was "cursed" and that somehow he had contributed to the deaths of these men, including to the death of his father. From that time on, he refused to ever meet, or even be near, another American president. Although invitations arrived from the White House and from other Washington social gatherings, he declined them all.

Was there truly a curse over Robert Lincoln's head? He certainly believed there was.

THE TRAGEDY OF CLARA HARRIS & MAJOR RATHBONE

Major Henry Rathbone, who was stabbed by Booth, recovered physically from the attack but would forever be haunted by the terrible night of the assassination. He and Clara soon married and moved to Germany, but the marriage was anything but blissful. Clara soon found that her husband was prone to bouts of depression and moodiness, none of which he had been inclined toward before the night in Ford's Theater. Then one morning, on Christmas Day of 1883, he went over the edge and killed Clara in a fit of insanity. Their children were spared, thanks to the bravery of their nanny, and Rathbone failed in his attempt to take his own life. He managed to stab himself four times, but lived long enough to die in a German mental institution in 1911.

The news of the tragedy soon reached Washington and rumors quickly spread. It was not long before the neighbors were crossing to the other side of the street, rather than walk directly in front of the former Rathbone house in Lafayette Square. A few people expressed concern that the troubled spirits of the family might return to their old home, while others insisted they already had. It was said that the sounds of a man's weeping, accompanied by the heartbreaking sobs of a woman and children, could be heard coming from the grounds. The stories would continue for many years but eventually, faded away.

But this was not the only story connected to Clara Harris and that tragic night at Ford's Theater. Following the assassination, the traumatized Clara returned home for a time and stayed with her parents at their house in Loudonville, New York, just north of Albany. Clara brought with her the gown that she had been wearing on the night Lincoln was killed, the fine fabric streaked and stained with the President's blood. In order to preserve the dress for all eternity, she is said to have placed it in a closet and then ordered the chamber to be walled shut.

As mentioned previously, Clara went on to lead a tragic life, ending in her murder at the hands of her once loving husband. Stories circulated for years that her weeping voice could be heard at the Rathbone's former home in Washington but it is at the cottage of her parents in Loudonville where her ghost is said to walk. Her hysterical specter has often been seen pacing the floors of the house and vanishing into the wall where the closet that held the bloody gown that was placed there so many years ago.

THE HAUNTINGS OF MARY SURRATT

Mary Surratt's trial was possibly one of the great travesties of American justice. She had been the proprietor of a Washington boarding house where John Wilkes Booth had stayed while plotting the kidnapping, and then murder, of Abraham Lincoln. At midnight, on the same night that Lincoln had been shot, Mary was rousted from her bed by police officers and Federal troops. She was accused of being a conspirator in Lincoln's death and was taken to the prison at the Old Brick Capitol. From that point on, Mary never stopped insisting that she was innocent and that she barely knew Booth, but no one listened.

The testimonies of two people were instrumental in Mary's conviction. One of them was a notorious drunk and the other was a known liar, a former police-man to whom Mary had leased her tavern in Maryland. At the trial's conclusion, she and three other defendants were found guilty and sentenced to death by hanging. Mary Surratt was the last of the four to die on July 7, 1865.

It is true that Mary may not have been as blameless as she claimed to be. Besides Booth, the other residents of the boarding house included her son, John, who was a Confederate courier, and several southern sympathizers. It is possi-ble that she knew more than she claimed to, but it is still doubtful that she was in any way involved in the murder plot. To say that the evidence against her was circumstantial is a gross understatement and in light of that, and other factors, the punishment certainly was much harsher than what was believed to be her crime.

Even though Mary Surratt was sentenced to die, the board which convicted her sent a petition to President Andrew Johnson to ask that her sentence be commuted to life in prison. Whether this is because she was a woman or because they had doubts about her guilt is unknown. The commander of the Federal troops in Washington was so sure that a last minute reprieve would arrive that he stationed messengers on horseback along the shortest route from the White House to the Washington Arsenal Prison, where the execution was to take place.

Until the time the hood was placed over her head, officials in charge of the execution were sure that Mary would be spared. While four of the defendants

Mary Surratt

died that day, three others received long prison sentences, including the famous Dr. Samuel Mudd. John Surratt, who had fled to Canada, was later returned for trial but was acquitted. What actually forced the hand of the judge to sentence Mary to death, and what stopped President Johnson from issuing the reprieve is unknown, because many historians today believe that Mary Surratt was innocent.

And it is possibly this injustice which keeps her spirit lingering behind...

In time, the Washington Arsenal Prison was converted into Fort Leslie McNair. In the courtyard on the north end of the fort is where the execution took place and is the spot where Mary and the other conspirators were cut down from the gallows and buried. They were later moved to permanent graves in other locations. There is an old story that maintains that Mary's spirit caused the sudden appearance of a boxwood tree on the spot where the scaffold once stood. It is claimed that the growth of the tree was her way of continuing to attract attention to her innocence.

The courthouse in which Mary was tried, and found guilty, was turned into an officer's quarters for the army base, while the courtroom itself became a five-room apartment. For years, it was reported that occupants of the apartment would hear the sounds of chains rattling throughout the rooms. According to records, the seven male defendants in the conspiracy trial were shackled together with chains and sat on a bench where the apartment is now located. Tradition holds that the reported sounds are these same chains, still echoing over the decades.

And sounds are not the only things reported. A number of residents of this apartment, and others which are located close to it, have claimed to see the apparition of a stout, middle-aged woman, dressed in black walking down the hallways of the officer's quarters. They have also heard the unexplainable sound of a woman's voice and have reported the sensation of being touched by an unseen hand. Could this be the ghost of Mary Surratt?

Within a few years of Mary's death, rumors began circulating that something strange was taking place at her former boarding house on H Street in Washington. Her daughter, Annie, had sold the house for less than half its value not long after her mother was executed, which is not really surprising considering the notoriety of the case.

But that may not have been the entire story. In the years which followed, the house was plagued with a rapid succession of new owners. People would move in and out very quickly, sometimes in a matter of months. Someone who worked for a newspaper got wind of the story and soon the local journalists began to interview the former owners --- after they got rid of the property, that is. Most of the accounts reported "strange sounds" and "whispers" in the building, voices that seemed to come from nowhere and which would be heard inside of rooms where no living person was present. It was also said that the phantom footsteps and creaking boards of the second floor were caused by the spirit of Mary Surratt, doomed to wander Washington until her name was cleared.

In the years that followed, the Surratt house was renovated many times, both inside and out, and recent owners claim that nothing of a "spirited" nature has taken place there in quite some time.

Mary's ghost is also said to frequent her home in Clinton, Maryland, located off of Brandywine Road. She is believed to be just one of the ghosts who haunt the place. John Wilkes Booth was said to have stopped at the tavern after making his escape from Washington, leading the tenant (and former policeman) to inform the authorities of Mary's part in the assassination. Many believe that he had other motives for wanting to see Mary convicted, leading most historians to question the accuracy of his statements to the authorities.

Stories of odd events at the tavern began in the 1940's when a widow lived in one half of the house and rented out the other. People spoke of seeing the ghost of Mary Surratt on the stairway between the first and second floors while others spoke of hearing men's voices, engaged in conversation, in the back of the house when no one was there.

In 1965, the site was taken over by the state and turned into a historical landmark. People who have worked and have visited there since claim to have seen apparitions of people in period clothing, have heard the phantom cries of children and footsteps pacing through the upper floor of the house when no one else was present.

THE GHOST OF DR. MUDD

On April 15, 1865, a loud pounding at the front door awakened Dr. Samuel Mudd from a deep sleep. He had been resting in one of the upstairs bedrooms of his farmhouse in Charles County, Maryland, about three miles from Beantown. No stranger to urgent calls in the middle of the night, the doctor hurried downstairs and opened his home to two men. One of them was badly in need of medical attention, so Dr. Mudd decided to allow them in.

Little did he know that this decision would not only entangle him in the Lincoln assassination conspiracy, but it would also make him a part of one of the greatest mysteries of the time. Was Dr. Mudd simply an innocent doctor, assisting an injured man, or did he aid John Wilkes Booth in his escape from Washington?

Dr. Mudd would later admit to the fact that he had met one of the late night callers, John Wilkes Booth, on an earlier occasion, but he claimed that on that April morning, he did not recognize him, nor his companion, David Herold. The two men were wearing makeshift disguises at the time and it is possible that Mudd truly did not recognize Booth. He would always maintain that he was simply administering to an injured man and that he was more interested in Booth's broken leg than in his identity.

Dr. Mudd proceeded to set Booth's leg and the two men were given food and rest until the afternoon of the same day. They left the house toward evening and headed toward Zekiah Swamp, reportedly never revealing their identities or how Booth came to be injured.

Several days later, Dr. Mudd was arrested for his alleged role in the Lincoln assassination. He was tried and convicted by the military court and was sentenced to life in prison at Fort Jefferson, located on Dry Tortugas Island in Florida. He remained there for four years, until he was pardoned by President Andrew Johnson. The pardon was not because of new evidence that proved Mudd to be innocent, but because of a request that had been signed by the warden, the officials and all of the inmates at the Florida prison. They believed they owed the doctor their lives after his aid during a Yellow Fever epidemic that swept through the prison.

There is still disagreement today over Mudd's role in the assassination. It is known that he was a southern sympathizer, as were most of the residents of southern Maryland, but it is also known that Federal officials "rushed to judgment" in the aftermath of Lincoln's death. They were anxious to catch anyone who might have been in any way involved in the murder and possibly innocent people like Dr. Mudd, and perhaps Mary Surratt, may have been caught in the frenzy.

In any case, Dr. Mudd's strongest supporters have been his descendants, who have fought to clear his name for many years. They have also made an effort to restore the Mudd farm house in Maryland and present it as a site of historical significance. Strangely enough, this effort was said to have been prompted by the ghost of Dr. Mudd himself.

According to Louise Mudd Arehart, the doctor's granddaughter, she had always been interested in the family history and in preserving the house but that interest was piqued when she began experiencing some rather strange events in the place. She began to hear knocking on the front door, but when she went to answer it, she found no one there. She also began to hear footsteps going up and down the stairs and in the hallways but again, she would find the areas to be empty when she would go to check.

Soon, she began to catch glimpses of a man on the grounds of the house. This odd figure was always dressed in black trousers, a vest and a white shirt with the sleeves rolled up to his elbows. After seeing him a few times, he also began appearing inside of the house, where she finally got a good look at him. She was convinced that the apparition was that of her grandfather, Dr. Samuel Mudd.

She became convinced that Dr. Mudd had returned to prompt her and her family to restore the old farm house, which had fallen into a state of disrepair. Thanks to her efforts, the house was listed on the National Register of Historic Places in 1974 and was opened to the public in 1983. Since then, the spirit of Dr. Mudd has only returned when restoration of the house slows down, or when it seems as though it is not proceeding to his expectations.

So, was Dr. Mudd guilty of conspiring in Lincoln's assassination? That question remains a mystery but perhaps it would provide the answers to his ghostly return. Perhaps he lingers here, not only to prompt the restoration of his home, but as a reminder of his innocence. Regardless, this is one of the only cases ever recorded where the intervention of a ghost was instrumental in the preservation of American history.

THE JUDGE'S GHOST

The aftermath of the Lincoln assassination conspiracy not only touched, and destroyed, the lives of the accused conspirators but the life of one of their accusers as well.

Judge Advocate General Joseph Holt was the presiding judge at the conspiracy trial and he was said to have been the only one of the panel who insisted on the death penalty for Mary Surratt. In the years which followed, we have to wonder if perhaps the judge grew to regret what many felt was a heartless decision because according to those who knew him, he changed dramatically after the trial.

Holt had apparently never been a popular man in Washington, even before the assassination. It was said that he was "taciturn, vindictive and ill-mannered" and all of this led to him being universally disliked. Attitudes toward Holt didn't change much after the trial either and he began to lead the life of a recluse. Newspaper articles from the period reported that he withdrew into his home and rarely saw, or spoke with, anyone. To further establish the fact that he was withdrawing from society, they also described his home as "decaying" with bars on the windows and heavy shades that did not permit outside light, nor the gaze of passersby, to venture inside. It was also said that the gardens of the house became tangled and overgrown and that people who walked along the street would often cross to the other side to avoid passing directly in front of the dilapidated mansion.

Holt spent his remaining years in almost total isolation, coming out only on occasion to buy food or to wander the few blocks to the Old Brick Capitol prison, where Mary Surratt had been imprisoned before her death. Here, he would stare at the barred windows for some time before returning to his house. Rumors began to spread that Holt lived in deep regret over his harsh punishment of Mary Surratt. It was also somehow learned, at least according to the local stories, that he spent hours reading and re-reading the transcripts of the conspiracy trial.

After Holt died, the new owners attempted to renovate the house and to remove some of the austere atmosphere of the place but to no avail. Soon after they took up residence, people in the neighborhood began to speak of the strange chill that pervaded various rooms of the house and the phantom sounds of someone pacing in the upstairs library. The stories maintained that the ghost of Judge Holt had remained within the house, still wracked with guilt over the terrible decision that he had been forced to make.

Years later, after the house had been torn down, another tale began making the rounds. In this version, people reported seeing the ghost of the Judge himself. It was said that he would appear on 1st Street, very near his former home, and walk along it to the Old Brick Capitol and then suddenly vanish.

What could the spirit have been seeking? Was it the truth of Mary Surratt's role in the conspiracy? Or merely absolution for the events that had taken place?

9. THE LINCOLN FUNERAL TRAIN

In the midst of all the clamor of Washington, the search for a killer, and the matter of getting a new president into office, there was another matter that needed to be attended to and that was Lincoln's funeral. The how and where of the service was decided by Edwin Stanton, as Mary had taken to her bed and Robert was still too stunned to be of much assistance.

The nation cried to see the fallen president and telegrams arrived from around the country asking to be the final resting place of President Lincoln. It was decided that Lincoln would be entombed beneath the dome of the Capitol building, a crypt which had originally been intended for George Washington, who was later moved to Virginia. Originally, Mary agreed to this plan, but soon changed her mind after being visited by a delegation of friends and officials from Illinois. It was decided that Lincoln would be taken back to Springfield for burial. It was a place which he always planned to go back to after leaving office. Unfortunately, he was not returning to Illinois in the way that he had planned.

Because of the national demand to see Lincoln one last time, it was decided that he would be taken to Springfield aboard a special train. This funeral train would follow a route through the east's major cities but first, they had to attend to the funeral service in Washington.

Never had any nation so mourned over a fallen leader. Not only Lincoln's friends but his scores of critics, who had mocked him in life, had ridiculed him as a baboon, had damned him as an ignorant backwoodsman, now lamented his death and grieved for the country. It was the first time in the history of America that a President had been felled by an assassin's bullet and this was seen as a tragic event in every corner of the Union.

The funeral services were planned for Wednesday, April 19, but Lincoln's adoring public was allowed to view the body the day before. The doors of the White House were opened on Tuesday and people crushed inside, inching past the body, weeping and speaking to the President, whose head lay on a white pillow with a faint smile frozen on his pale and distorted face. By the end of the day, an estimated 25,000 people had crowded past the mahogany coffin.

On Wednesday, Lincoln's body was again resting in the East Room, which was now hushed and dim and draped in yards and yards of black crepe. Upstairs, Mary was locked in her room, too deranged from grief and hysterical weeping to attend the services. Lizzie Keckley and Tad tried to console her. Though stricken himself, Tad would throw his arms about his mother's neck and plead with her: "Don't cry so, Momma! Don't cry, or you will make me cry too! You will break my heart!" But it was no use, Mary was simply too crazed to be able to pull herself together.

Services began around eleven that morning, with more than 600 people crowded into the East Room. Robert, his face ashen and grave, was wearing his Captain's uniform and he stood at the foot of the coffin. He tightly held the hand of his little brother and Tad trembled, his face swollen with tears. General Grant, a black mourning band on one arm, sat alone at the other end, staring at a cross of lilies. He began to cry, unable to believe what had happened. He would always maintain that this was the saddest day of his life. By now, nearly all of Washington was there, including President Andrew Johnson and his Cabinet, Sumner and his Congressional colleagues, numerous military officials, Lincoln's personal cavalry escort and bodyguards, Nicolay, Hay, mayors and government delegates from across the country.

Four different ministers spoke and prayed for Lincoln and after that, twelve reserve corps sergeants carried his casket out to the funeral car. As they stepped out into the bright, sunlit day, church bells all over the city began to toll. From the forts that still surrounded the city, cannons began to boom. Throngs of people lined Pennsylvania Avenue and thousands more peered from windows and roofs along the parade route. Many of these people had been in position for hours, waiting for Lincoln's casket to appear. Federal troops moved into formation to accompany the hearse, which now waited outside the White House. The coffin was placed on a high platform, surrounded by glass and elevated so that everyone could see. Soon, the hearse moved forward, pulled by six white horses, all festooned with black cloth and decoration. The procession moved in a slow, measured cadence, a detachment of Black troops in the lead. The hearse was followed by a riderless horse, befitting a fallen general, and all walked to the steady muffled beat of drums. The lines swelled with wounded soldiers, who left their hospital beds and marched along now, ignoring their pain as they hobbled after their slain leader. There was a procession of Black citizens, walking in lines that stretched from curb to curb, holding hands as they walked along.

Lincoln's body was then carried to the Capitol Building and placed in the rotunda. An honor guard took up position around it and remained in place until the next morning. Shortly after the sun appeared, wounded soldiers were allowed to file past the casket and pay their final respects. After this, the viewing was opened to the public once more. The crowds were so large that the soldiers outside had to remove wooden barricades around the building so that no one would be injured. It was said that over 3,000 people per hour filed past the coffin before the doors were finally closed at midnight.

Noah Brooks, a Washington correspondent for a California newspaper and frequent visitor at the White House, described the scene: "Directly beneath me lay the casket in which the dead President lay at full length, far, far below; and like black atoms moving over a sheet of gray paper, the slow-moving mourners, seen from a perpendicular above them, crept silently in two dark lines across the pavement of the rotunda, forming an ellipse around the coffin and joining as they advanced toward the eastern portal and disappeared."

On April 21, a nine-car funeral train, decorated with Union flags, waited at the Baltimore & Ohio depot as a hearse carried Lincoln from the Capitol. Earlier, some men had removed the coffin of Willie Lincoln from his tomb and had placed it in the funeral car. They now placed Lincoln beside his beloved son and the train crawled forward with ringing bells, beginning a 1,600-mile journey back to Illinois.

Over the course of the next fourteen days, the train steamed north and then westward, passing through perhaps the greatest crowds ever assembled in America. Reporters followed its passage, telegraphing details to their newspapers back home of the strange, circus-like atmosphere surrounding the funeral train. It is believed that 7 million northerners looked upon Lincoln's hearse or coffin and that 1.5 million actually looked upon his silent face. Ninety different funeral songs were composed in his honor while thousands (or even millions) cried, fainted, took to their beds, and even committed suicide in the frenzy of Lincoln's passing.

The train arrived first in Baltimore, where a hard rain had started to fall. As in Washington, guns boomed and church and firehouse bells tolled. The schedule only allowed Lincoln to remain in the city for four hours, so thousands jammed the train tracks, hoping for a glimpse of the President's coffin. The casket was removed from the train and the pallbearers had to elbow their way through streets jammed with people, many of whom were selling funeral crepe and photographs of Lincoln. The coffin was placed in what Baltimore newspapers called "the most beautiful hearse ever constructed", made from genuine rosewood, gilded and fitted with a back and two sides of French plate glass. The procession of military and civic representatives was so large that it took three hours to get to the Merchant's Exchange, where the coffin was opened for viewing. It was believed that nearly 10,000 people looked on Lincoln but thousands more were turned away, disappointed that the funeral train had to be on its way. There was no argument and no one to intercede for those turned back or for the long lines of schoolchildren who stood patiently in the rain for a last look at the President.

As the train passed through Pennsylvania, people began to line the tracks and watch it pass. Little towns were filled in honor of the president and local bands played funeral dirges as the train went by. The old and sick were carried to the stations to see the train pass by and babies were held up high to see the "black choo-choo". Only at the station in York did the train make a stop. The ladies of the town had made an urgent request and the train halted for six of them to enter the funeral car and place a cartwheel of red, white and blue flowers on Lincoln's coffin.

In Harrisburg, thousands waited all night in the rain for a glimpse of Lincoln the following morning. Unfortunately, violent thunderstorms had descended on the city but despite the rain, the massive crowds still came. Jagged streaks of lightning crossed the sky as church bells rang and cannons thundered. The crowds followed the hearse and its military escort to the House of Representatives at the State Capitol, where a black-draped catafalque was waiting. The procession took so long that the casket was not opened for viewing until 9:30 that evening. Thousands passed in a double line until the next morning when the funeral train once again prepared to leave. Before the casket was closed though, the undertaker had been forced to re-chalk Lincoln's face to hide the growing discoloration. Lincoln had become America's first public embalming and it would be some time before the methods of preservation would be perfected. In addition, the body also had to be dusted --- the coffin had been opened and closed so many times that the President's face and beard had started to attract dust particles from the air.

It was still raining the next morning but more than 40,000 people still jammed the streets to watch the procession as the casket was returned to the funeral train. At a few minutes after eleven, the train steamed out of Harrisburg toward Philadelphia. It headed east through the countryside and moved slowly through Lancaster, where an enormous crowd had erected a huge sign that read: "Abraham Lincoln, the Illustrious Martyr of Liberty, The Nation Mourns His Loss. Though Dead, He Still Lives".

In Philadelphia, more than 500,000 people were already waiting at Independence Hall when the train arrived. It was in Philadelphia that a new aspect was added to the viewing of Lincoln --- violence. For the first time, people were actually hurt in the frantic crush to get into Independence Hall and see the President's body. The trip into the city had been orderly. Thousands had come out beside the tracks to stand in silence, or kneel as many did, while the train passed. All the shops had closed and farms stood silent and deserted in honor. For miles before the Philadelphia station though, there were no gaps in the crowd, just solid lines. The train arrived at Broad Street station in late after-oon, more than two hours ahead of schedule, but then the careful organization of the city officials began to go to pieces.

It took nearly two hours to get the procession under way but afterward, the city would claim that they offered the most gigantic display of all. Eleven divisions marched to the inevitable booming of cannons, tolling of bells, firing of guns, roll of muffled drums and eerie funeral dirges. At the square, when the Old State House was passed, a large transparency was uncovered --- a picture of Lincoln with a background of a huge coffin, spectacularly lighted by gas jets that formed letters that spelled out "He Still Lives". The coffin was carried to the East Wing of Independence Hall, where the Declaration of Independence had been signed.

The viewing that night was by invitation only and handpicked people had been given cards by the mayor. These special guests were stopped at 1:00 a.m. and as they departed, they passed long lines of the general public, which were already forming to be admitted four hours later. The exhausted throngs waited all night and by Sunday morning, the entire city was on edge. When pickpockets began to terrorize a portion of the line, it surged into a mob, pressing against the guide ropes. Then the ropes were cut --- by "villains" the newspapers later said --- and bedlam broke out. People who had been almost to the doors were sent back by the police to the end of the nearly three-mile-long double lines to wait for another six or seven hours. The crowd surged out of control and the police fought to keep order. Bonnets were pulled from women's heads and their hair turned loose, dresses were torn away and ripped, all to a chorus of women's screams. As many of the young women fainted, they had to be extricated from the lines and passed over the people's heads. One woman had her arm broken and word got out that two little boys were dead but were finally revived. The closer people got to Lincoln, the more impassioned they became. The police refused to let people stop for even a second to view the body, insisting that they keep moving at all times. Even with these precautions, a number of women tried to climb over the wooden barricade to touch the President or to kiss his face.

It was all finally over at 1:00 a.m. on Monday morning and the casket was returned to the train. It steamed on toward New York, where ceremonies had begun the day before. The entire city, it seemed, had been draped in black and in the hours before the train's arrival, , the streets of the city became impassable. The police and military fought to keep them open, but it was no use.

In the early morning darkness of Monday, April 24, the train stopped in Trenton, New Jersey for about half an hour. Trenton was wounded because it was the only state capital on the route where Lincoln was not taken from the train and funeral services held. The people stood and stared as the train pulled into the station and one observer noted that "it did not occur to the male part of the throng that a general lifting of the hat would have been a silent but becoming mark of respect to the dead." Far different, he noted, at Newark, where every man removed his hat and feelings were so deep that women also removed their bonnets out of respect.

The train arrived in Jersey City at 10:00 a.m., where crowds had been gathering since early morning. Only ladies and their escorts were allowed into the gallery at the depot, where the large clock had been stopped at 7:22 a.m., the precise moment of Lincoln's death. When the train arrived, a German singing group thundered forth with a funeral dirge. New York had been building a magnificent hearse but it would have been risky to ferry it across the Hudson so the coffin was sensibly transferred to a small hearse and carried across the river. A second ferry took the train's funeral car, with Willie's casket in it, and a third took the big car that carried the official escort that journeyed through to Springfield. Here in New York, a new engine, a new pilot engine and seven cars would be supplied by the new line, the Hudson River Railroad.

The body of Lincoln was taken to City Hall and more than 600,000 spectators accompanied it while more than 150,000 stood in line for a glimpse of the president. The honor guard had a full-time job on their hands trying to keep people from touching Lincoln and trying to keep women from kissing his face and hands. Although no rioting broke out as it did in Philadelphia. The police had their hands full with surging crowds, most of whom were beaten back with clubs, and with pickpockets, who freely roamed the area, stealing at will. Only one thing happened to break the boredom of the wait - someone threw a light cigar at the black festoon just under a huge banner proclaiming "The Nation Mourns". Flames rose high for a moment but a brave officer climbed up and tore down the mass of burning material and others stamped out the fire on the stone steps.

That night, after the doors were closed, the embalmer brushed a heavy coating of dust from Lincoln's face, beard and clothing. They also rearranged his facial features, which had become twisted from exposure.

At some time on Monday, a New York photographer named Gurney took photos of Lincoln's cadaver and sent proofs to Mary in Washington. He planned to make the photo available for sale within a few days but Mary objected. It was said that she was shocked by the "unnatural" expression on her husband's face. When he heard that a photograph had been taken, an outraged Edwin Stanton ordered the plates be broken and the photo destroyed. A number of telegrams were sent begging Stanton to reconsider, but he refused. The plate was eventually destroyed but not before Stanton was sent a copy of the photo to show how unobjectionable it was. The photo ended up being lost in Stanton's papers for years and was later sent to the Illinois State Historical Library. It was found in 1952 by a student who was researching Stanton's files.

The final procession back to the train became New York's moment of glory.

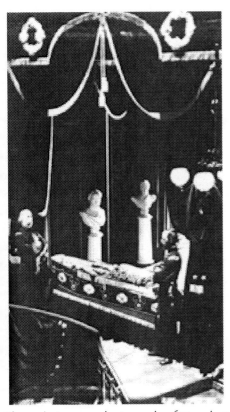

The only known photograph of Lincoln in death. The plates were ordered destroyed by Edwin Stanton but one copy survived in his files. (Illinois State Historical Society)

Peter Relyea, the official undertaker for the city of New York, had been issued a special permit to accompany Lincoln's body to Springfield. For three days, he had been building an elaborate funeral car before marveling crowds on the city streets. He had been living and sleeping in the car, trying to get it finished before the procession. Now, just in the nick of time, he led the hearse into the park enclosure in front of City Hall. The hearse, pulled by 16 gray horses, nearly paralyzed all who saw it. Its platform was huge --- fourteen feet long and almost seven feet wide --- and on the roof of the canopy was a gold and white Temple of Liberty with a half-masted flag on its crown. Inside of the canopy was white fluted satin that matched the inside trimmings of the coffin and hanging down from it, so that it would hang directly above the casket, was a glittering gilt eagle with its wings spread. It was said to be an amazing work of art and would remain the most elaborate creation on the funeral route.

An hour later, Lincoln was placed aboard the Relyea creation and the procession began to move. Led by a squad of mounted police, who made sure the route was clear, it started off with a hundred dragoons with black and white plumes and red, yellow and blue facings on their uniforms. They were followed by military officers and their staffs and then the magnificent hearse. Behind that were more than 11,000 soldiers, Irishmen in bright green with black rosettes in their lapels, Zouaves with baggy red trousers and black ribbons on their chests, military and government representatives from foreign countries and eight divisions of civilians. One of them was made up from the trades --- cigar-makers, waiters, cooks clerks, carpenters and others --- and there were divisions of medical men, lawyers, members of the press, the Century Club, the Union League, Freemasons, Civic Societies and finally, nearly 300 Black men.

The procession took nearly four hours to pass each point on its route. The streets were jammed with spectators and it was said that window seats could be rented for $50 from those who lived in the apartment buildings along the path. At Chamber Street, a shaggy St. Bernard dog trotted out from the crowd and walked alongside the hearse for a block or so. A whisper spread that the dog and his master had recently paid a visit to Lincoln at the White House and the President had kindly patted the dog on the head. A spurious legend? Or could the dog have known who he trotted next to in the amazing hearse?

All through the afternoon, church bells and fire bells tolled, bands wailed, guns boomed and people wept for the great and fallen leader. Eventually, the train moved on to Albany, leaving thousands disappointed. Many who did not get a chance to see the president boarded trains and planned to try again in Chicago or in Springfield. The Illinois delegates, who were accompanying the train, realized in horror just how many people could be descending on the small city. One of the delegates hurried to Springfield to prepare for the worst.

After leaving the city, the train steamed across the countryside toward Albany. It passed scores of small towns along the way, where people gathered to watch it pass. Each of the towns had gone to enormous trouble to build a display, an arch or to inscribe a huge motto for the train as it passed. At towns where there was no station, there was often a minister and his parishioners, kneeling or singing a hymn. At Yonkers, the people lined up and the men all raised their hats. At Tarryton, a gathering of young women appeared, all dressed in white, save for black sashes, creating an effect both chaste and mournful. At Peekskill, the train stopped as a band played a dirge and guns fired. At Poughkeepsie, the train made another stop. The hilltop here was black with people, guns were fired and church bells and fire bells clanged with a fury .It was now growing dark and as the train continued on toward Albany, torches and bonfires illuminated the tracks. It was approaching midnight when the train entered the capital. The coffin was carried to the State House and all through the night, the residents of Albany and the neighboring countryside passed by it.

The next day, there was another procession but this time, the 300 people accompanying the train, except for a portion of the military, went straight to two hotels where the city had arranged them to be lodged. They were worn out both physically and emotionally from the never-ending mourning ceremony and there were still six more funerals ahead of them. Albany had been there first chance to really rest on the route so far.

At noon on Wednesday, April 26, Albany's grand parade got under way with a specially built catafalque, marchers, bands, tolling bells and huge crowds of people. It was a grand event but was not the type of "circus" that Albany crowds had been expecting. Van Amburgh's traveling menagerie was in town and had been planning to offer a parade and celebratory show to entertain the crowds when the assassination occurred. The circus owner, Van Amburgh, quickly proclaimed: "There will be no exhibition given until the President's remains have left the city and the grand parade scheduled for this morning will be postponed until tomorrow."

Albany was probably the only one of the funeral cities that had the chance to pick up its spirits so rapidly after being drenched in sorrow. The train soon rolled out of the city and moved on to Buffalo, the only city on the list that was likely disappointed by the arrival of the President's body. A short time earlier, on the day of the Washington funeral, Buffalo's citizens, grieving at the news of the assassination, were not content to simply hold church services. Instead, the people put on their own mock funeral, just as though the coffin and body had been there. They had built a magnificent catafalque, had a huge procession, offered

The city of Buffalo had a mock funeral prior to the arrival of the President's body but huge mobs turned out for the real thing.

prayers and eulogies and had gone through the motions as if the real thing was taking place. Then when they got the news that their city had been chosen to hold a funeral on the procession route, there was, along with a feeling of pride, a bit of a letdown as well. Buffalo had exhausted its first frenzied extravagance during the mock ceremony, although citizens assured themselves that having the real thing would be many times better. Somehow though, when the time came, it wasn't.

They used the same magnificent hearse car with its six white horses, draped in black and the well-attended viewing was held in St. James Hall, with the coffin up-tilted and brilliantly lit. Thousands filed past the coffin but between the dirges, the silence was oppressive and the "utter decorum" and "remarkable order" were somehow not as much of a tribute as the wild straining to get near the coffin or to touch the President's hand, as had occurred in other cities.

The train continued on through New York and into Ohio. The overnight trip from Buffalo passed through lines of silent people, with continuous bells and bands and displays of maidens all dressed in white with black sashes. At Westfield, the engine stopped for water in the early morning hours and five young ladies were allowed to bring a cross of flowers into Lincoln's funeral car. They knelt and each in turn kissed the coffin. Kissing the coffin, with it solid barrier of wood and lead, was a desperately futile gesture but it never failed to move those who watched to tears.

Vast crowds stood on the hills outside of Cleveland as the train passed beneath prepared arches that bore sad inscriptions. Of all of the funerals held Cleveland's was the strangest so far. The funeral was both a solemn wake and a theatrical pageant of flowers, with the city showing its appreciation for the American President by introducing an Oriental note to the proceedings. In the city park, a huge Chinese pagoda was erected for Lincoln's coffin to be displayed on for what turned out to be more than 100,000 mourners.

The train arrived on the outskirts of Cleveland in the early hours of Friday, just one week since it had left Washington. As it moved slowly into the city, officials on board the train saw crowds of people on the hillsides and high up, a young girl draped in a flag under an archway that read "Abraham Lincoln". The train pulled into the station and was greeted by a 36-gun salute and thousands of onlookers. People had flocked to the city from all over northern Ohio, western Pennsylvania and eastern Michigan and boatloads of them had arrived by water from Detroit. All of the ladies in attendance had been warned to leave the hoops for their skirts at home --- the breakage of such attire by the throng, officials said, would be swift and total. With the thousands in attendance however, standing in the pouring rain, there was not a hint of disorder.

Legions of marchers and mourners descended on the city park, with its Chinese Pagoda for the President. The idea of the outdoor ceremony turned out to be an inspiration because thousands more were able to view the body than would have been possible in any building. When ceremonies were completed, Lincoln's body was loaded back onto the train and it set off for Columbus.

The city of Columbus also offered a funeral of flowers. People had roses in their hands, which they tossed under the wheels of the hearse as it passed and invalid soldiers from the Soldier's Hospital had literally covered the street near the hospital for several hundred yards with lilac blossoms.

The Columbus hearse was a somber vehicle, drawn by six white horses, but it did have one aspect to it that would have amused Lincoln himself. On one side of the dais, in silver, block letters, was the name "Lincoln". The President tried whenever possible to avoid the obvious. When in the Spring of 1864 he had been asked to sign a letter presenting a sword to General Dix, Lincoln signed his name and then was asked to add "President of the United States". His answer, putting down his pen, was "Well, I don't think I'll say 'this is a horse'." When the coffin was placed on a dais at the State Capitol building, the platform was noticed to have been also fitted with the same helpful identification. Lincoln would have gotten a chuckle out of this bit of tragic absurdity.

The Columbus procession moved through drapes and flowers and mottos from the city to the sounds of guns firing, bells ringing and the muffled beat of drums. The hook and ladder car of the fire department carried 42 young ladies on it, all singing hymns. The coffin was placed on the dais, which had no canopy and no flags. However, instead of black velvet, the surface of it was a carpet of moss and tender green leaves, which let off a fragrant aroma as the casket sank into it. The people gathered in the rotunda watched in awe as the undertaker unscrewed the coffin lid, made a slight adjustment to the position of the body and then made a motion that the viewing could begin. People began to stream by and for the first time, their passing was in complete silence. A carpet had been laid in the hall so that the shuffling of feet and the click of shoe leather would not be heard. For the eighth time, thousands and thousands of Americans said goodbye to their fallen President.

From Columbus, the train steamed on toward Indiana. At Woodstock, there were 500 citizens waiting beside the tracks and a contingent of young women were allowed to board the train and lay flowers in the funeral car. At Urbana, more than 3,000 people surrounded a huge, floral cross as the train steamed on toward Indiana. At Richmond, Indiana, the church bells of the town rang for an hour as the train arrived and over 15,000 people greeted the funeral with pantomimes, scenes and stage effects that must have looked both ghastly and somewhat horrifying to the party looking out from the railroad car windows. One such display featured a beautiful young woman who was illuminated by red, white and blue lights over a mock coffin, creating one of the most eerie displays on the funeral train's journey.

The train reached Indianapolis near midnight, arriving during a torrential rainstorm. At first, it was hoped that if the rain stopped, the procession could go on during the afternoon. However, the rain continued to fall, increasing in power from minute to minute, until the black decorations on every house hung soggy and the black dye formed dark streaks on the front of stone buildings. Reluctantly, the huge Indianapolis procession had to be canceled and the time devoted to it was set aside for viewing instead. All of the way from the train depot to the State House, soldiers were lined up at attention, forming two long lines of blue uniforms and drawn swords. The hearse was pulled by eight white horses, six of which had pulled Lincoln as the president-elect a few years before. They took the coffin into State House square and under a large arch to which portraits of Lincoln, Indiana Governor Oliver Perry Morton, General Grant, General Sherman and Admiral Farragut had been affixed. On the points of it were busts of George Washington, Daniel Webster, Henry Clay and Lincoln. The busts were all crowned with laurel wreaths.

The first to view Lincoln were 5,000 Sabbath School scholars and the last were the Colored Masons and hundreds of African-American citizens who all carried with them copies of the Emancipation Proclamation. The casket lay under a black velvet canopy, which was sprinkled with golden stars. The mourners all saw a coffin that was heaped with flowered crosses and wreaths, which is interesting in itself. Here, on this epic cross-country journey, an American tradition was created. Prior to Lincoln's funeral, it was not customary to send flowers to funerals. With the death of a beloved President, many people searched their hearts about the best way to express their sympathy and thousands of them decided upon flowers. Although with the best of intentions, the sheer numbers of flowers sent to Lincoln were greatly overdone, emptying the contents of each city's hothouses. The colors ran heavily to red, white and blue, which would have pleased a President who stated that he felt emotional each time he looked at the flag. In Springfield, there would be a tremendous red heart, covered with thousands of red roses, that would travel with the coffin all of the way to the tomb.

When the viewing was completed, the coffin was escorted back to the train with Governor Morton and most of the population of Indianapolis following behind. The governor had greeted and entertained Lincoln when he was traveling to Washington as the president-elect and he watched his casket leave the state with great sorrow.

With Indianapolis behind, the train steamed on toward Illinois. There was a massive funeral planned in Chicago and then, it would go on to Lincoln's home town in Springfield. But due to an unexpected delay, there was to be one more funeral, an impromptu service at the depot in Michigan City, Indiana. The funeral train was supposed to travel straight through and arrive in Chicago during the late morning hours of Monday, May 1. But it was forced to wait for one hour in Michigan City for a committee of more than 100 important men from Chicago who were coming out to escort the train into the city. The residents of Michigan City made the most of the unexpected stop, especially since the rain of the past few days had cleared to brilliant sunshine. Now, the occupants of the train were greeted by the depot arch of evergreens and roses, decorated with black ribbons and "tasteful" portraits of Lincoln.

The 300 weary mourners that traveled with the funeral were taken off the train for a large breakfast in the station. After that, the rule was broken about not opening the coffin except in the cities that were putting on funerals. The townspeople were allowed to pass through the car and view Lincoln and then a small funeral service was held with young women singing hymns.

Abraham Lincoln had always been among the first to alter procedures and break rules on the spur of the moment for something better. His office hours were always flexible and he often received people at all hours of the day and night. He was the bane of all who tried to protect his time from the people. The people wanted so little, he often said, and there was so little that he could give - he must see them. Because of this, the Michigan City meeting with the people would have gladdened Lincoln's heart.

A short time later, Lincoln was almost home. As the train steamed into Chicago, he was finally entering the great city of his home state, which had been a prairie mudhole when he first settled in Illinois and now was a rich and crowded city of more than 300,000. Although a few years away from the Great Fire that would change the city forever, Chicago was already claiming its place as one of the greatest cities in America. Lincoln had many ties with the city. He had spent a lot of time there pleading cases as a lawyer and it was in Chicago that his presidential nomination was garnered. And it was in Chicago that, just before the famed Lincoln-Douglas debates began in 1858, Lincoln and Stephen Douglas spoke to large audiences on successive July nights, gaining the attention of newspapers and readers across the country.

It was to this magnificent city that Lincoln's body came on Monday, May 1, 1865. It had traveled more than 1,500 miles to reach this point and the hearts of the people who awaited him in Chicago were heavy.

The funeral train did not go the entire distance on the Illinois Central tracks to the

The city of Chicago held one of the grandest funerals along the entire route of the Lincoln Train

Union Depot but stopped on a trestle that carried the line out in the lake some distance from the shore. The train arrived in silence, save for the ringing of its bell. A temporary platform had been built, with steps leading down to the ground, and from there, a Veteran Guard carried the coffin the short distance up the street to where a platform was waiting beneath a dramatic Gothic, three-section arch. The city had employed three distinguished architects, and had spent more than $15,000, to create the arch, design the hearse and build the decorations for the Court House. Thirty-six young women walked beside the platform that carried the president and they showered flower petals in all directions. The streets were packed with over 100,000 people as excursion trains had been coming into the city for more than 24 hours, carrying curiosity-seekers from the east. Thousands lined up at the courthouse in the rain and mud to see Lincoln. Exhausted soldiers and police officers recalled that the lines moved less than one foot per hour on Monday and Tuesday. More trains arrived, bringing more people to add to the chaos as at least 125,000 lined up to view the casket.

Ambulances came and went, carrying injured onlookers and women who faint-ed from grief and exhaustion. At one point, a section of wooden sidewalk gave away and plunged hundreds into the mud and water below.

The route of the funeral procession ran through what was the most elegant section of town. It passed down Michigan Avenue first, then along Lake Street, then along Clark to Court House Square, avoiding the world's largest stockyards, the McCormick Reaper Works and the flour mills. On each side of the hearse walked six pallbearers, each of them old friends of Lincoln. Marching second on the left hand side was "Long John" Wentworth, the mayor of the city. Standing six feet, six inches in height, he had started off in Congress as a Democrat but later became a Republican and a staunch supporter of Lincoln. When Wentworth was elected the mayor of Chicago in 1857, he made cleaning out crime and cor-ruption his top priority. The story went that the rough and tumble candidate once made a one-sentence campaign speech from the front steps of the Court House --- "You damn fools, you can either vote for me or go to hell."

The procession in Chicago was much as it had been in other cities. There was a legion of clergy with white crosses adorning their black armbands and a division of Zouaves in baggy red pants. There was also a group of captured Confederate soldiers who had taken the oath and now belonged to the Union Army. They were followed by a troop of more than 10,000 schoolchildren, walk-ing with saddened faces and wearing black ribbons in their hair, along with sashes, armbands and badges. In the procession were also immigrants from Germany, France, Ireland and Eastern Europe. They were butchers, bricklayers, tailors and carpenters, all carrying banners with clumsily worded but unmis-takably heartfelt messages about the President. The parade was followed up with a humble, yet unwanted, procession of "colored citizens".

When the hearse finally arrived at the city's Court House, the great bell in the tower began to ring so loudly that it could be heard in the farthest reaches of Chicago. It was not until early evening that the doors were opened to the pub-lic and the viewing went on all night long and all through the following day. It was believed that more than 7,000 people per hour passed by the coffin for a quick viewing of the President.

The light in the Court House was kept purposely dim but there was a gen-eral feeling that the discoloration that had been present under Lincoln's eye from the bullet wound was starting to spread over his entire face. The continual application of white chalk was no longer able to hide the dark stains. It had been in New York that the blackness had really started to distress the mourners but now, the body was starting to look even worse. Lincoln had started to shrivel, making it appear as though his coffin was many sizes too big for him. To many, his cheeks seemed hollow and his face much more gaunt than it had been in life. The reporters had been positive that after New York, there would be no more pen casket viewings but constant care and powdering had managed to keep the body in a decent condition. Even so, the undertaker was glad that Chicago was nearly the last stop on the route.

At around 8:00 p.m. on Tuesday evening, the great procession re-formed and by the light of 10,000 torches, the eight black horses drew the hearse with Lincoln's coffin on it back to the railroad depot. The train finally began the last leg of its journey on that night, leaving Chicago and passing under arches which were illuminated with bonfires and decorated with sentiments like "Coming Home", "Bear Him Home Tenderly" and "Home is the Martyr".

The sun came up on the funeral train as is reached Atlanta and then steamed on towards the south. Emotions ran high aboard the train as it reached Lincoln, a town that had actually been named for the President when he was still a young lawyer. In 1853, Lincoln had been called upon to draft the town's incorporation papers and the founders decided to name the place in his honor. Lincoln responded to the suggestion with his usual humility: "I think you are making a mistake," he said. "I never knew of anything named Lincoln that ever amounted to much." Lincoln then presided over the town's dedication and on April 27, the official story has it that he poured out juice from a watermelon to christen the ground but other stories say that he spit out a mouthful of seeds as a christening instead. Knowing Lincoln's sense of humor, the latter is probably correct.

The train steamed into Springfield at just before 9:00 in the morning and was greeted by a mass of people at the station and on the surrounding rooftops. They met the train in silence. Only the sound of weeping could be heard. It seemed the entire city of Springfield had been draped in black but two of the most important buildings to be decorated with mourning weeds was the old State House in the center of the town square, where the body would be placed for public viewing and the home that Lincoln had owned and lived in for nearly 16 years. The house now belonged to the Tilton family. Lucien A. Tilton was the president of the Great Western Railway and over the four years of their occupancy, had been kept busy by an estimated 65,000 people who had visited the home and had asked to tour it. Mrs. Tilton was rather apprehensive about what might happened during the Lincoln funeral but she was a kind-hearted person and had already resolved herself to the fact that she was going to allow people to take grass from the yard, flowers from her garden or leaves from the trees. She had no idea what was coming --- by the end of the funeral services, her lawn and gardens had been stripped, paint had been scraped from her house and bricks had been carried away from her retaining wall as souvenirs.

The rotunda of the State House had been draped in black cloth and the second floor House of Representatives, where Lincoln was to lie in state, had been renovated so that the speaker's podium had been removed to allow more people to pass through it. The columns inside had been draped with black and banners and signs decorated the interior. At the center of the room, a catafalque had been built to hold Lincoln's coffin. The catafalque was one of the most amazing of the entire funeral route. Its canopy was "Egyptian" in design with columns and "half-Egyptian" suns depicted between the columns. It was 24 feet high and more than 10 feet long. The top was made from black broadcloth and at the tops of the columns were black plumes with white centers, hiding large eagles. The inside roof of the canopy was blue, spangled with silver stars.

On the morning of May 3, the public viewing was scheduled to begin and thousands of people began to gather outside of the State House. Long before the imposing procession arrived from the station, huge, motionless lines began to form away from the north gate. Time ticked by and soon, people began to grow restless --- but there was an unavoidable delay inside. When the undertakers had opened the coffin upstairs, even these hardened professionals were shocked. Thomas Lynch was a courtesy undertaker for the occasion and he had been invited to assist Dr. Charles D. Brown, Lincoln's embalmer. The doors of the room were locked and Dr. Brown, in great distress, informed the other man that he had no idea how to remedy the condition of Lincoln's face - which had turned totally black.

According to Lynch's account: "I asked to have the body turned over to me and the other undertaker readily consented. Making my way with difficulty through the crowds which thronged the corridors of the State House, I called at a neighboring drugstore and procured a rouge chalk and amber, with such brushes as I needed, and returned to the room. I at once set about coloring the President's features, placing the materials on very thick so as to completely hide the discoloration of his skin. In half an hour, I had finished my task and the doors were thrown open to the public."

The crowds were admitted shortly after 10:00 a.m. and they walked upstairs to the House of Representatives, were sorted out by guards and were sent in groups past Lincoln's casket. Everyone was afforded a few moments to look inside and then they were ushered out through the exit and down the stairs. Before they left, they were asked to make a donation to the Lincoln Monument fund. Very few of those who filed past the coffin shed any tears. They were too shocked by what they saw. But outside on the street, they broke down and wept. Over the next 24 hours, thousands streamed past the coffin but these were not the hysterical crowds of New York and Chicago, these were the folks that Lincoln had known and loved in life. They were the people he talked to in the street, laughed with, ate with and the people he had missed while living in Washington. They were now the people who wept in the streets of the city that he called home.

On the morning of May 4 , the last service was held in Springfield. Robert

Lincoln had arrived and had left his mother in Washington with Tad. She had not yet risen from her bed and missed the country's frantic farewell to Lincoln completely.

Shortly before the service, Dr. Charles Brown worked to make Lincoln presentable for one last occasion, dressing him in a clean collar and shirt and applying more powder to his face. He finished just before the procession formed outside. The procession included Robert Lincoln, who rode in a buggy with members of the Todd family; John Hanks, one of Lincoln's only remaining blood relatives; elderly Sarah Lincoln; Thomas Pendel, Lincoln's door man from the White House, and a representative of the household servants; and Billy, Lincoln's black barber and friend.

The final parade was presided over by General Joseph Hooker and he led "Old Bob", the tired and rider-less horse whom Lincoln had ridden the law circuit on. The parade, like the others before it, was long and marked with music, banners and signs. The journey was to end two miles away at quiet Oak Ridge Cemetery, traveling over what were then rough, country roads. From time to time, bands broke out in dirges, including four newly composed "Lincoln Funeral Marches", and when the music was silent, all that could be heard was the unbroken and ominous roll of drums. Finally, the procession wound under the evergreen arch at the cemetery's entrance, down through the little valley between two ridges, along the small stream and to the receiving tomb that was half-embedded in the hillside. It stood with its iron gates and heavy new vault doors open to receive the President. With no delay, the coffin was carried from the hearse and placed on the marble slab inside of the vault. As soon as the hearse and horses moved away and let the people come in close, it could be seen that there were two coffins on the slab. The small casket of Willie Lincoln had been brought to the vault first and was waiting for his father to arrive.

People were standing and sitting behind the tomb on the hillside and along the valley in front of it, with the brook, swollen by the Spring rains, dividing the audience. Robert Lincoln stood grimly on one side of the tomb and Ward Hill Lamon, stood nearby. Lamon had stayed close to the President's body all of the way west, skipping meals and acting as if he were still protecting his old friend from danger. He alternated between helpless weeping and helpless rage over the fact that he had not been present that night at Ford's Theater. On this day in May 1865, Lamon cried unashamedly at the fate of Abraham Lincoln.

As the service began, Reverend A.C. Hubbard began to read Lincoln's words from his second inaugural address. As it drew to a close, Bishop Matthew Simpson of the Methodist Church rose to give his funeral oration. The Bishop's voice was shrill and harsh and people found it unpleasant but the sound was forgotten when they listened to the words that he spoke of their friend and fallen leader. He spoke so eloquently that people applauded parts of the sermon. When he was finished, a hymn was sung and then Dr. Gurley, who had officiated at the funeral in Washington, delivered the benediction. A final hymn was sung, the words printed on black-edged cards that were distributed throughout the audience, and then the gates to the tomb were closed and locked. The key to the tomb was handed to Robert Lincoln, who passed it to his cousin, John Todd Stuart, who would become the guardian of the President's body for many years to come.

When the lock turned in the door of the President's tomb, the seemingly endless days of travel and the grand spectacles were finally over. Lincoln was laid to rest in Oak Ridge Cemetery in the holding crypt while his tomb and monument were constructed.

But he would not rest in peace for some years to come. No one knew it at the time, but the days, months and years of travel for President Lincoln's body were just beginning.

The Funeral Train across the country was an unprecedented event in American history. Millions had seen the body, had attended services or had simply stood and watched as the train passed by. It is no wonder that the Lincoln Funeral Train has become an object of legend --- or that many eerie tales have been attached to its passing.

For many years, a phantom funeral train has been reported traveling the same route as the Lincoln train did back in 1865. The first sightings of the train were in New York but soon spread westward into Ohio, Indiana and Illinois. One of the earliest reports of the ghost train appeared in the Albany, New York Evening Times. An article appeared that stated: "Regularly in the month of April, about midnight, the air on the tracks becomes very keen and cutting. On either side of the tracks it is warm and still. Every watchman when he feels the air, slips off the track and sits down to watch. Soon the pilot engine of Lincoln's funeral train passes with long, black streamers and with a band of black instruments playing dirges, grinning skeletons all about.

"It passes noiselessly. If it is moonlight, clouds come over the moon as the phantom train goes by. After the pilot engine passes, the Funeral Train itself with flags and streamers rushes past. The track seems covered with black carpet, and the coffin is seen in the center of the car, while all about it in the air and on the train behind are vast numbers of blue-coated men, some with coffins on their backs, others leaning upon them.

"If a real train were passing its noise would be hushed as if the phantom train rode over it. Clocks and watches would always stop as the phantom train goes by and when looked at are five to eight minutes behind. Everywhere on the road about April 27, watches and clocks are found to be behind."

The story of the Phantom Train passed into local and regional lore in many locations along the route of the original Lincoln Funeral route. Many of the sto-ies are still told, even in areas where the railroads have since faded into oblivion, disuse and abandonment. Legends still tell of a phantom train that appears in late April, steaming along tracks that no longer exist.

In other places, where the tracks are still in use but have long since been taken over by companies that did not even exist in 1865, the stories also tell of a phantom train. One such place is Chicago, where one of the most impressive funerals was held for the fallen President. According to Ursula Bielski, author of the book *Chicago Haunts*, the train is still believed to make an appearance each year in the early part of May, the anniversary of the Funeral Train's arrival in the Windy City.

"The tracks where the Lincoln Funeral Train came into Chicago are now used by the Metra Line, which brings commuters back and forth to the city from Indiana, along Lake Michigan," Ursula explained. "They are still an important part of the train's lore because around every May 1, it's not unusual to find history buffs, Civil War buffs and ghost hunters literally camped out around what used to be the Illinois Central tracks. They are waiting for a glimpse of the famous train and many claim that haven't been disappointed."

Ursula's haunted tours of Chicago often pass the site of the old tracks and she and her other guides usually mention the phenomenon. "It's always been a long standing tradition that whenever the train passes, clocks and watches along the tracks always stop and never work again," she said. "With that in mind, I always remind people to be careful about what watch they wear when they come looking for the phantom train."

10. SECRETS OF THE GRAVE

Springfield had gotten news of the assassination of Abraham Lincoln by telegraph less than an hour after the event had occurred. Ned Baker, editor of one of the local newspapers and a friend of Lincoln's, ran from his office on North Sixth Street to the house where another Lincoln friend, James Conkling, lived and knocked urgently on the door. Conkling came down from bed and then weeping, went upstairs to tell his family. The news was in every home in the city before dawn and soon, groups of people began to gather in the square near the newspaper offices. There was a low murmur of talk, of grief, anger and revenge, but when the final notice came that it was all over, silence fell over the crowd. No one whispered, or even moved --- they simply began to cry.

Within the hour though, the people began to stir and the shocked City Council met and began forming a plan to take to the citizens. A mass meeting was held at noon and it was decreed that Springfield was going to try and assure that the assassinated President be laid to rest in the city that he had called home. Fortunately for Springfield's wishes, the newly elected Governor Oglesby and Richard Yates, the wartime governor and recent Senator, were both friends of Lincoln and were both in Washington. They had been among the last of Lincoln's visitors on April 14. Through Robert Lincoln, they made an appeal to Mary, who was locked in her bedroom, that Illinois loved her late husband and that his body should be returned home to rest among his friends and neighbors. Mary however, was torn between the fact that she had quarreled with just about all of her old friends and her family in Springfield and never wanted to set foot there again, and the sincere desire to choose a burial place that would have been her husband's choice. Up through the day of the Washington funeral, she insisted that Chicago was her first choice and her second was the crypt that had been built for Washington under the rotunda of the Capitol building. Her husband had promised her that after he left the Presidency, they would make a tour of

Europe and then retire in Chicago and so she favored a quite burial place near Lake Michigan. It appealed to her that he would be buried close to the resting place of his old adversary, Stephen Douglas. Of course, Mary had not been to Chicago since Douglas' death and did not know that his grave was desolate and after four year, had no monument to mark it.

But Mary also looked back at her last days with Lincoln and realized again that he had a foreshadowing of his own death. "You will see Europe, but I never shall," he told her. She also remembered her husband's dream to live once more in Springfield. She also recalled his saying, just a few weeks before his death, that he wanted to be buried in "some quiet place". He also said, back in 1860, that the new Springfield cemetery was one of the most beautiful spots that he had ever seen. The day of the cemetery's consecration was a grand event in the city and just about everyone in Springfield walked the two miles to Oak Ridge in an informal procession. What they saw was a great contrast to the graveyard within the city limits called "Hutchinson's Cemetery". It was run for profit by John Hutchinson, who made furniture and sold coffins to those interred within his grounds. Hutchinson's was almost filled to capacity at the time of Oak Ridge's consecration and the new burial ground was badly needed for the growing city. The authorities were prepared to buy Hutchinson out and remove the bodies to Oak Ridge but this took some time and for years afterward, Oak Ridge remained mostly woods, hills and unbroken forest.

After agonizing over her decision, Mary finally decided that Oak Ridge was the "quiet place" that Lincoln would have wanted and directed that his coffin be placed in the public receiving tomb until a proper site could be chosen for his monument. Her decision was telegraphed to Springfield and days and nights of frantic preparation were made. Mary wanted Lincoln to be buried at Oak Ridge --- but the city of Springfield had other plans.

As it happened, when the body of President Lincoln arrived in Springfield, he actually had two different graves waiting for him. One of the graves was a temporary vault at remote and wooded Oak Ridge, which Springfield officials believed was no place to bury a fallen hero, and the other was a small hill located in the heart of the city. This spot was called Mather's Hill and it had been the site of the magnificent stone house that was owned by Thomas Mather. Builders were employed to work around the clock and convert the house into a tomb, complete with a handsome vault and stone urns on either side of the entrance.

Mary learned of the downtown tomb through "troublemakers" and sent a telegram stating that her husband absolutely was to be buried at Oak Ridge. Springfield officials remembered the Mrs. Lincoln of old and recalled her erratic nerves and fits of temper, so they tried to be very diplomatic with the widow. They telegraphed Edwin Stanton and told him that her wishes would be respected --- but kept right on with the work at the Mather tomb. They simply could not believe that Mary would want her husband buried out in the woods and even if she did, they were sure that they could change her mind when she arrived in Springfield. Regardless of this, they did make the other preparations that she and Robert asked for, namely moving Eddie Lincoln's body from Hutchinson's Cemetery and placing it in the vault at Oak Ridge. When the Funeral Train finally arrived in the city, Lincoln's body, along with Willie's, was also securely locked into the vault.

Although Springfield officials had placed Lincoln at Oak Ridge, they still had no intention of leaving him there. In Washington, Mary's friends were urging her to return Lincoln to the Capitol dome, while in Springfield, plans marched ahead to place the president in the Mather tomb. In fact, plans had already been started for a huge ceremony to mark the occasion.

Mary was furious when she read in the newspapers of Springfield's intentions. Immediately, she sent word and threatened to remove Lincoln's body from the city if a monument was not built at Oak Ridge. She claimed that she would further have him removed back to Washington if they did not cooperate. Oak Ridge, she declared, was where her husband would have wanted to rest.

In the Summer of 1865, Mary moved to Chicago and a delegation from Springfield went up to plead with her again. She refused to see them and at last, they surrendered. A temporary vault was built for Lincoln at Oak Ridge and in seven months, on December 21, he was placed inside. Six of Lincoln's friends wanted to be sure the body was safe, and a plumber's assistant named Leon P. Hopkins made an opening in the lead box for them to peer inside. All was well and Lincoln and his sons were allowed a temporary rest.

The new construction on a permanent tomb would last for more than five years and the catacomb would actually be completed first. It was constructed with five vaults inside and about two months before Lincoln was moved inside, one of the vaults was filled. His son, Tad, had died in Chicago at the age of 18 and had been placed in the monument. Soon, preparations were made to move Lincoln, as well as Willie and Eddie, into the catacomb as well.

It was during this time that strange things began to be reported in the vicinity of Lincoln's resting place. A short time before the bodies were to be moved into the new monument, Springfield residents and curiosity-seekers began to tell of a spectral image that was seen near the crypt. It was believed to be Lincoln himself, investigating the construction site where he and his sons were to be laid to rest.

Even after the move was completed, the eerie stories continued. Inside of the monument, strange sobbing noises and what sounded like footsteps began to be reported as well. Many of the locals believed that the ghost of President Lincoln was haunting Oak Ridge Cemetery and the new tomb.

Some believe that he still walks here today.

On September 19, 1871, the caskets of Lincoln and his sons were removed from the hillside crypt and taken to the catacomb. The tomb was not quite finished yet, but the completed portion was a suitable place for them to be moved to. The plumber, Leon P. Hopkins, opened the coffin once more and the same six friends peered again at the President's face.

During the move, it was noticed that Lincoln's mahogany coffin was beginning to deteriorate, so his friends brought in a new iron coffin, to which the inner coffin of lead, containing Lincoln's body, was transferred. The dead President was laid to rest again, for another three years, while the workmen toiled away outside. Once more though, his rest was interrupted.

On October 9, 1874, Lincoln was moved again. This time, his body was placed inside of a marble sarcophagus, which had been placed in the center of the semi-circular catacomb. A few days later, the monument was finally dedicated. Money had been raised for the groups of statues which were situated outside and the citizens of Springfield seemed content with the final resting place of their beloved Abraham Lincoln. But then a new threat arose from a direction that no one could have ever predicted.

The events that unfolded next began ironically in Lincoln, Illinois. Although most who lived there had no idea, the city had become a hide-out for a gang of counterfeiters run by a man named "Big Jim" Kneally. The place was an ideal refuge for Kneally's "shovers", pleasant-looking fellows who traveled around the country and passed, or "shoved", bogus money to merchants.

At some point, in the Spring of 1876, business turned bad for the Kneally gang. Their supply of counterfeit money had dwindled because their master engraver was serving a 10-year sentence in Joliet prison. The engraver, Benjamin Boyd, had been little more than a petty criminal before turning his artistic skills to making plates for counterfeit money. A relentless agent of the Chicago office of the Secret Service, Captain Patrick Tyrell, pursued Boyd through five states and for eight months before finally arresting him in Fulton, Illinois.

Needless to say, with his engraver locked away, things were looking grim for Kneally's business. That was when he seized on a plan. He would have his men kidnap a famous person and for a ransom, negotiate for the release of Boyd from Joliet prison. Strangely, the famous personage that Kneally planned to kidnap was Abraham Lincoln --- or at least his famous corpse.

In June, Kneally began putting the scheme into action. He sent five of his men into Springfield to open a saloon that could be used as a base of operations for the gang. Meanwhile, Kneally returned to St. Louis, where he owned a legitimate business, so that he could be far away from suspicion as events unfolded and have an airtight alibi. The saloon soon opened as a drinking establishment and dance hall. One of the men, Robert Splain, served as a bartender while the rest of the gang loitered there as customers. They made frequent visits to the Lincoln Tomb at Oak Ridge, where they found the custodian, John C. Power, more than happy to answer questions about the building. On one occasion, he innocently let slip that there was no guard at the tomb during the night. This clinched the last details of the plan, which involved stealing the body and spiriting it away out of town. It would be buried about two miles north of the city, under a Sangamon River bridge, and then the men would scatter and wait for Kneally to negotiate the ransom.

It was now early June, about a month before the plan was to be carried out, and the men had little to do but wait around the saloon and drink. One night, one of the men got very drunk and spilled the details of the plan to a prostitute, who worked at a nearby "parlor house". He told her to look for a little extra excitement in the city on the night of July 4. He and his companions planned to be stealing Lincoln's body while the rest of the city was celebrating the holiday. The story was too good to keep and the woman passed it along to several other people, including the city's Chief of Police, Abner Wilkinson, although no record exists how these two knew one another. The story spread rapidly and Kneally's men disappeared.

Kneally didn't give up on the plan however. He simply went looking for more competent help. He moved his base of operations to a tavern called the Hub at 294 West Madison in Chicago. Kneally's man there was named Terence Mullen and he operated a secret headquarters for the gang in the back room of the tavern. One of Kneally's operatives, Jack Hughes, came into the Hub in August and learned that a big job was in the works. Kneally wanted to steal Lincoln's corpse as soon as possible. Hughes and Mullen had no desire to do this by themselves, so they brought another man into the mix. His name was Lewis Swegles and he had a reputation for being one of the most skilled grave robbers in Chicago. They decided he would be perfect for the job.

In 1876, grave robbery was still a national horror and would remain that way for some years to come. Illinois, like most other states, had no laws against the stealing of bodies. It did however, have a statute that prevented selling any bodies. Needless to say, this put medical schools into dire need. They often had to depend on "ghouls", or grave robbers, to provide corpses for their anatomy classes. These "ghouls" had become the terror of communities and friends and relatives of bereaved families sometimes patrolled graveyards for several nights after a funeral, with shotguns in hand.

Swegles came in and discussed the ins and outs of grave robbery with the other two men and they quickly devised a plan. They would approach the Lincoln monument under the cover of night and pry open the marble sarcophagus. They would then place the casket in a wagon and drive northward to the Indiana sand dunes. This area was still remote enough to provide a suitable hiding place for however long was needed.

Swegles, being the most experienced of the group, agreed to everything about the plan except for the number of men needed. He believed the actual theft would be harder than they thought and wanted to bring in a famous criminal friend of his to help them. The man's name was Billy Brown and he could handle the wagon while the others pillaged the tomb. The other two men readily agreed.

On November 5, Mullens and Hughes met with Swegles in his Chicago home for a final conference. They agreed the perfect night for the robbery would be the night of the upcoming Presidential election. The city would be packed with people and they would be in downtown Springfield very late, waiting near the telegraph and political offices for news. Oak Ridge Cemetery, over two miles away and out in the woods, would be deserted and the men could work for hours and not be disturbed. It would also be a perfect night to carry the body away, as the roads would be crowded with wagons and people returning home from election celebrations. One more wagon on the road would not be noticed.

The men agreed and decided to leave for Springfield on the next evening's train. Swegles promised to have Billy Brown meet them at the train, but felt it was best if he didn't sit with them. He thought that four men might attract too much attention.

Hughes and Mullen conceded that this was a good idea, but wanted to at least get a look at Brown. Swegles instructed them to stay in their seats and he would have Brown walk past them to the rear car. As the train was pulling away from the station, a man passed by the two of them and casually nodded his head at them. This was the mysterious fourth man. Brown, after examination, disappeared into the back coach. Hughes and Mullen agreed that he looked fit for the job.

While they were discussing his merits, Billy Brown was hanging onto the back steps of the train and waiting for it to slow down at a crossing on the out-skirts of Chicago. At that point, he slipped off the train and headed back into the city. You see, "Billy Brown" was actually Agent Nealy of the United States Secret Service.

Lewis Swegles was actually a government informant who had been putting together other charges against Hughes and Mullen for Patrick Tyrell, the Secret Service officer who had captured Ben Boyd. When he learned of the body-snatching plan, he began boasting of his grave robbing prowess to get more details about the plan and then brought the information to Tyrell, who had already been using Swegles' information for a counterfeiting case against the two men. Tyrell had instructed Swegles to go along with the plan and included his own man as "Billy Brown".

As Nealy was slipping off the train, more agents were taking his place. At the same time the conspirators were steaming toward Springfield, Tyrell and a half-dozen operatives were riding in a coach just one car ahead of them. They were also joined on the train by a contingent of Pinkerton detectives, who had been hired by Robert Lincoln after he got word of the plot to steal his father's body. The detectives were led by Elmer Washburne, one of Robert's law partners.

A plan was formed between Washburne and Tyrell. Swegles would accompany the grave robbers to Springfield and while assisting in the robbery, would signal the detectives, who would be hiding in another part of the monument. They would then capture Mullen and Hughes in the act.

When they arrived in Springfield, Tyrell contacted John Todd Stuart, Robert's cousin and the head of the new Lincoln National Monument Association, which cared for the tomb. He advised Stuart of the plan and together, they contacted the custodian of the site. The detectives would hide in the museum side of the monument with the custodian. This area was called Memorial Hall and it was located on the opposite side of the structure from the catacomb. They would wait there for the signal from Swegles and then they would rush forward and capture the robbers.

The first Pinkerton arrived just after nightfall. He carried with him a note for John Power, the custodian, which instructed him to put out the lights and wait for the others to arrive. The two men crouched in the darkness until the other men came inside. Tyrell and his men explored the place with their flash-lights. Behind the Memorial Hall was a damp, dark labyrinth that wound through the foundations of the monument to a rear wall of the catacomb, where Lincoln was entombed. Against this wall, in the blackness, Tyrell stationed a detective to wait and listen for sounds of the grave robbers. Tyrell then returned to the Museum Room to wait with the others. Shortly after complete darkness had fallen outside, their wait was over.

A lantern flashed outside the door and sounds could be heard as the grave obbers worked at the lock. Almost immediately, Mullen broke the saw blade that he was using on the lock and so they settled in while he resorted to the long and tedious task of filing the lock away. After some time, Mullen finally removed the lock and opened the door to the burial chamber. Before them, in the dim light, they saw the marble sarcophagus of President Lincoln. Now, all they had to do was to remove the lid and carry away the coffin --- which turned out to be much harder than they had anticipated. The stone was too heavy to move, so using an ax, they broke open the top, then moved the lid aside and looked into it. Swegles was given the lantern and was stationed nearby to illuminate the work area. Left with no other option, he complied, although he was supposed to light a match at the door to alert the Secret Service agents that it was time to act. He had no idea how he was going to do that. Meanwhile, Mullen and Hughes were busy lifting out the heavy casket. Once this was completed, Mullen told Swegles to go and have the wagon moved around. He had assured Mullen and Hughes that Billy Brown had it waiting in a ravine below the hill.

Swegles raced around to the Memorial Hall, gave the signal to the detectives, and then ran outside. Tyrell whispered to his men and, with drawn revolvers, they rushed out and around the monument to the catacomb. When they got there, they found the lid to the sarcophagus was moved aside and Lincoln's casket on the floor --- but the grave robbers were gone!

The detectives scattered outside to search the place. Tyrell ran outside and around the base of the monument, where he saw two men near one of the statues. He whipped up his pistol and fired at them. A shot answered and they fought it out in a hail of gunfire, dodging around the monument. Suddenly, one of the men at whom he was shooting called out Tyrell's name --- he was firing at his own agents!

Mullen and Hughes had casually walked away from the tomb to await the return of Swegles, Brown and the wagon. They never suspected the whole thing had been a trap. They had only wanted to get some air and moved into the shadows where they wouldn't be seen in case someone wandered by. After a few minutes, they saw movement at the door to the tomb and had started back, thinking that Swegles had returned. They heard the pistol shots and saw a number of men around the monument. They took off running past the ravine and vanished into the night. Assuming that Swegles had been captured, they fled back to Chicago, only to be elated when they found him waiting for them at the Hub tavern. He had returned with the horses, he told them, but found the gang gone. He had came back to Chicago, not knowing what else to do, to await word of what had happened. Thrilled with their good fortune, the would-be grave robbers spent the night in drunken celebration.

The story of the attempted grave robbery appeared in the newspaper following the Presidential election but it was greeted with stunned disbelief. In fact, only one paper, the Chicago Tribune, would even print the story because every other newspaper in the state was sure that it was not true. To the general public, the story had to be false and most believed that it had been hoaxed for some bizarre political agenda. Most people would not believe that the Secret Service and Pinkerton agents would be stupid enough to have gathered all in one room where they could see and hear nothing, and then wait for the criminals to act. The Democrats in Congress charged that the Republicans had hoaxed the whole thing so that it would look like the Democrats had violated the grave of a Republican hero and in this way, sway the results of the election. To put it bluntly, no one believed that Lincoln's grave had been, or ever could be, robbed!

The doubters became believers on November 18, when Mullen and Hughes were captured. The newspapers printed the story the following day and America realized the story that had appeared a short time before had actually been true. Disbelief turned into horror. Letters poured into the papers, laying the guilt at the feet of everyone from the Democrats, to southern sympathizers, to the mysterious John Wilkes Booth Fund.

The people of Illinois were especially outraged and punishment for the two men was bound to be severe, or it would have been had the law allowed it. After their arrest, the conspirators were under heavy guard in the Springfield jail and on November 20, a special grand jury was convened in Springfield and returned a bill against Mullen and Hughes for attempted larceny and conspiring to commit an unlawful act. There was nothing else they could be charged with. Grave robbery was not a crime in Illinois and the prosecution, bolstered by Chicago lawyers dispatched by Robert Lincoln, could find no grounds to charge them with anything other than the minor crimes of larceny and conspiracy. Ironically, the charge was not even for conspiring to steal President Lincoln's body. It was actually for planning to steal his coffin, which was the property of the Lincoln National Monument Association.

The public was aghast at the idea that these men would get off so lightly, even though the grand jury had returned a quick indictment. Continuances and changes of venue dragged the case along to May of 1877, when it finally came to trial. The jury was asked by the prosecution to sentence the men to the maximum term allowed, which was five years in prison. On the first ballot, two jurors wanted the maximum, two of them wanted a two-year sentence, four others asked for varying sentences and four others even voted for acquittal. After a few more ballots, Mullen and Hughes were incarcerated for a one-year stay in Joliet.

It did not take long before the story of the Lincoln grave robbery became a hotly denied rumor, or at best, a fading legend. The custodians at the site simply decided that it was something they did not wish to talk about anymore. Of course, as the story began to be denied, the people who had some recollection of he tale, created their own truth in myths and conspiracies. The problem in this case however, was that many of these "conspiracies" happened to be grounded in the truth.

Thousands of people came to see the Lincoln burial site and many of them were not afraid to ask about the stories that were being spread about the tomb. From 1876 to 1878, custodian John C. Power gave rather evasive answers to anyone who prodded him for details about the grave robbery. He was terrified of one question in particular and it seemed to be the one most often asked: Was he sure that Lincoln's body had been returned safely to the sarcophagus after the grave robbers took it out? Power was terrified of that question for one reason -- because at that time, Lincoln's grave was completely empty!

On the morning of November 8, 1876, when John Stuart learned what had occurred in the tomb the night before, he rushed out to the site. He replaced the casket and then repaired the marble of the sarcophagus. He was not able to rest after the incident, fearing that the grave robbers, who had not been caught at that time, would return and finish their ghoulish handiwork. So, he made a decision. He notified the custodian and told him that they must take the body from the crypt and hide it elsewhere in the building. Together, they decided the best place to store it would be in the cavern of passages that lay between the Memorial Hall and the catacomb.

That afternoon, Adam Johnson, a Springfield marble-worker, took some of his men and they lifted Lincoln's casket from the sarcophagus. They covered it over with a blanket and then cemented the lid back into place. Later that night, Johnson, Power and three members of the Memorial Association stole out to the monument and carried the 500-pound coffin around the base of the obelisk, through Memorial Hall and into the dark labyrinth. They placed the coffin near some boards that had been left behind in the construction.

The following day, Johnson built a new outer coffin while Power set to work digging a grave below the dirt floor. It was slow work, because it had to be done between visitors to the site and he also had a problem with water seeping into the hole. Finally, he gave up and simply covered the coffin with the leftover boards and wood. For the next two years, Lincoln lay beneath a pile of wood in the labyrinth, while visitors from all over the world wept and mourned over the sarcophagus at the other end of the monument. More and more of these visitors asked questions about the theft. They were questions full of suspicion, as if they knew something they really had no way of knowing.

In the Summer and Fall of 1877, the legend of the tomb took another turn. Workmen arrived at the monument to erect the naval and infantry groups of statuary on the corners of the upper deck. Their work would take them into the labyrinth, where Power feared they would discover the coffin. The scandal would be incredible, so Power made a quick decision. He called the workmen together and swearing them to secrecy, showed them the coffin. They promised to keep the secret, but within days everyone in Springfield seemed to know that Lincoln's body was not where it was supposed to be. Soon, the story was spreading all over the country.

Power was now in a panic. The body had to be more securely hidden and to do this, he needed more help. He contacted two of his friends, Major Gustavas Dana and General Jasper Reece and explained the situation. These men brought three others to meet with Power. They were Edward Johnson, Joseph Lindley and James McNeill, all of Springfield.

On the night of November 18, the six men began digging a grave for Lincoln at the far end of the labyrinth. Cramped and cold, and stifled by stale air, they gave up around midnight with the coffin just barely covered and traces of their activity very evident. Power promised to finish the work the next day.

These six men, sobered by the responsibility that faced them, decided to form a brotherhood to guard the secret of the tomb. They brought in three younger men, Noble Wiggins, Horace Chapin and Clinton Conkling, to help in the task. They called themselves the Lincoln Guard of Honor and had badges made for their lapels.

The city of Springfield got their first look at the Guard during the funeral of Mary Todd Lincoln in July 1882. At the ceremony, the men conducted themselves so mysteriously that people whispered questions about who they were. It was assumed that the men concealed some great secret about the Lincoln family and rumors flew.

After the funeral, John T. Stuart told the Guard that Robert Lincoln wanted to have his mother's body hidden away with his father's. So, late on the night of July 21, the men slipped into the monument and moved Mary's double-leaded casket, burying it in the labyrinth next to Lincoln's.

Visitors to the tomb increased as the years went by, all of them paying their respects to the two empty crypts. Years later, Power would complain that questions about Lincoln's empty grave were asked of him nearly everyday. Finally, in 1886, the Lincoln National Monument Association decided that it was time to provide a new tomb for Lincoln in the catacomb. A new and stronger crypt of brick and mortar was designed and made ready.

The press was kept outside as the Guard, and others who shared the secret of the tomb, brought the Lincoln caskets out of the labyrinth. Eighteen persons who had known Lincoln in life filed past the casket, looking into a square hole that had been cut into the lead coffin. Strangely, Lincoln had changed very little. His face was darker after 22 years but they were still the same sad features these people had always known. The last man to identify the corpse was Leon P. Hopkins, the same man who had closed the casket years before. He soldered the square back over the hole, thinking that he would be the last person to ever look upon the face of Abraham Lincoln.

The Guard of Honor lifted the casket and placed it next to Mary's smaller one. The two of them were taken into the catacomb and lowered into the new brick and mortar vault. Here, they would sleep for all time.....

"All time" lasted for about 13 more years. In 1899, Illinois legislators decided the monument was to be torn down and a new one built from the foundation. It seemed that the present structure was settling unevenly, cracking around the "eternal" vault of the president.

There was once again the question of what to do with the bodies of the Lincoln family. The Guard of Honor came up with a clever plan. During the 15 months needed for construction, the Lincoln's would be secretly buried in a multiple grave a few feet away from the foundations of the tomb. As the old structure was torn down, tons of stone and dirt would be heaped onto the grave site both to disguise and protect it. When the new monument was finished, the grave would be uncovered again.

When the new building was completed, the bodies were exhumed once again. In the top section of the grave were the coffins belonging to the Lincoln sons and to a grandson, also named Abraham. The former President and Mary were buried on the bottom level and so safely hidden that one side of the temporary vault had to be battered away to reach them.

Lincoln's coffin was the last to be moved and it was close to sunset when a steam engine finally hoisted it up out of the ground. The protective outer box was removed and six construction workers lifted the coffin onto their shoulders and took it into the catacomb. The other members of the family had been placed in their crypts and Lincoln's was placed into a white, marble sarcophagus.

The group dispersed after switching on the new electric burglar alarm. This device connected the monument to the caretaker's house, which was a few hundred feet away. As up-to-date as this device was, it still did not satisfy the fears of Robert Lincoln, who was sure that his father's body would be snatched again if they were not careful. He stayed in constant contact with the Guard of Honor, who were still working to insure the safety of the Lincoln's remains, and made a trip to Springfield every month or so after the new monument was completed. Something just wasn't right. Even though the alarm worked perfectly, he could not give up the idea that the robbery might be repeated.

He journeyed to Springfield and brought with him his own set of security plans. He met with officials and gave them explicit instructions on what he wanted done. The construction company was to break a hole in the tile floor of the monument and place his father's casket at a depth of 10 feet. The coffin would then be encased in a cage of steel bars and the hole would be filled with concrete, making the president's final resting place into a solid block of stone.

On September 26, 1901, a group assembled to make the final arrangements for Lincoln's last burial. A discussion quickly turned into a heated debate. The question that concerned them was whether or not Lincoln's coffin should be opened and the body viewed one last time? Most felt this would be a wise precaution, especially in light of the continuing stories about Lincoln not being in the tomb. The men of the Honor Guard were all for laying the tales to rest at last, but Robert was decidedly against opening the casket again, feeling that there was no need to further invade his father's privacy. In the end, practicality won out and Leon P. Hopkins was sent for to chisel out an opening in the lead coffin. The casket was placed on two sawhorses in the still unfinished Memorial Hall. The room was described as hot and poorly lighted, as newspapers had been pasted over the windows to keep out the stares of the curious.

What actually took place in that room is unknown except from the reports of the select few who were present. Most likely, they were the same people who had been present several years before when the body had been placed in the brick and mortar vault.

A piece of the coffin was cut out and lifted away. According to diaries, a "strong and reeking odor" filled the room, but the group pressed close to the opening anyway. The face of the president was still covered with a fine powder of the white chalk, which had been applied in 1865 before the last burial service. Lincoln's features were said to be completely recognizable. The casket's headrest had fallen away and his head was thrown back slightly, revealing his still perfectly trimmed beard. His small black tie and dark hair were still as they were in life, although his eyebrows had vanished. The broadcloth suit that he had worn to his second inauguration was covered with small patches of yellow mold and the American flag that was clutched in his lifeless hands was now in tatters. There was no question, according to those present, that this was Abraham Lincoln and that he was placed in the underground vault. The casket was sealed back up again by Leon Hopkins, making his claim of years ago to be true --- he really was the last person to look upon the face of Lincoln.

The casket was then lowered down into the cage of steel and two tons of cement was poured over it, forever encasing the president's body in stone.

This should be the end of the story but with all lingering mysteries, a few questions still remain. The strangest are perhaps these: Does the body of Abraham Lincoln really lie beneath the concrete in the catacomb? Or was the last visit from Robert Lincoln part of some elaborate ruse to throw off any further attempts to steal the president's body? And did, as some rumors have suggested, Robert arrange with the Guard of Honor to have his father's body hidden in a different location entirely?

Most historians would agree that Lincoln's body is safely encased in the oncrete of the crypt but rumors persist that say otherwise. Whose word do we have for the fact that Lincoln's body is where it is said to be? We only have the statement of Robert Lincoln, his friends and of course, the Guard of Honor. They were, without question, an honorable and loyal groups of men but weren't these the same individuals who left visitors to the monument to grieve before an empty sarcophagus while the president was actually hidden in the labyrinth, beneath a few inches of dirt?

In addition to the mysteries that still remain about Lincoln's burial site, here are also the lingering stories of his ghost. There are many, perhaps thanks to the first Lincoln ghost stories that claimed he walked back and forth from his temporary burial site to the unfinished tomb, who claim that Lincoln's ghost haunts the monument at Oak Ridge.

Many have reported that someone here does not rest in peace. Many tourists, staff members and historians have had some unsettling impressions here that aren't easily laughed away. Usually these encounters have been reported as the sound of ceaseless pacing, tapping footsteps on the tile floors, whispers, quiet voices and the sounds of someone crying or weeping in the corridors. But are these sounds and eerie feelings really caused by a lingering spirit -- or a haunting of another sort?

Perhaps the most common type of haunting that exists is what is called a "residual haunting", when events literally "impress" themselves on the atmosphere of a location. These events then replay themselves, like a recording, when conditions are right. The alleged haunting at Lincoln's Tomb may be the result of just this sort of manifestation. Based on the number of grieving visitors who have come to the Monument over the years, from agonized friends to mournful strangers, it's possible that all of this emotion may have left an impression behind. This impression may be what so many have experienced here over the years.

11. THE
HAUNTED
WHITE HOUSE

I sit in this old house, all the while listening to the ghosts walk up and
down the hallway. At four o'clock, I was awakened by three distinct knocks on
my bedroom door. No one was there. Damned place is haunted, sure as
shootin'!
PRESIDENT HARRY S. TRUMAN

There is no doubt that few presidents left the sort of mark on the White
House that Lincoln did. His impact on the history of America has been immeas-
urable and in 1864, when he sought re-election, he did so with the idea that his
plans were unfinished. When he was assassinated, his plans for reconciliation
between the North and South were interrupted and his work was left incomplete. In fact, some would say that it remains incomplete, even today. Perhaps
this is why his spirit is so often reported at the White House and may explain
why he is our nation's most famous ghost.

Although there are few reports of Lincoln's specter haunting the White
House of the late Nineteenth Century, there is nothing to suggest that his spirit
was not present. In the years following his death, staff members and residents
often reported mysterious footsteps in the hallways. However, one of the earliest
reliable reports from someone who actually saw Lincoln's apparition came from
President Theodore Roosevelt, who took up residence in the house nearly forty
years after Lincoln's death. "I see him in different rooms and in the halls," he
admitted. In truth, it comes as no surprise that Roosevelt may have "attracted"
the ethereal presence of Lincoln as he greatly admired the former leader and
quoted his speeches and writings often.

During the terms of President Calvin Coolidge, his wife Grace actually ncountered Lincoln. She stated that he was dressed "in black, with a stole draped over his shoulders to ward off the drafts and chills of Washington's night air". She explained that one day as she passed by the Yellow Oval Room, she was startled to see Lincoln staring out the window in the direction of the Potomac, his hands behind his back. Lincoln turned and looked momentarily in her direction and then vanished. During his tenure in the White House, the room had been Lincoln's library and he often stood at the same window, looking out with his thoughts filled with the course of the war. At that same window, Lincoln's spirit has also been seen and felt by others, including the poet and Lincoln biographer, Carl Sandburg. He also stated that he felt Lincoln's presence close to him in the Yellow Oval Room.

President Herbert Hoover also admitted to hearing mysterious sounds in the White House. Although he never acknowledged that it was Lincoln's ghost, Hoover left no doubt that he had heard something in the darkened corridors that he could not explain.

By the time that Franklin Delano Roosevelt began his long series of terms as President, Lincoln had been dead for nearly 70 years. However, his ghost remained, unwilling or unable to leave the White House. During FDR's administration, Lincoln was at his most active, perhaps because of the concerns about the perilous state of the nation during the time of the Great Depression and World War II.

Eleanor Roosevelt told reporters that she had never seen Lincoln, but she admitted that she had felt his presence late at night when she used the Lincoln bedroom as a study. She often said that she sensed him "standing behind her, peering over her shoulder". She also admitted that she sometimes heard his "footsteps in the second-floor hallways". Mrs. Roosevelt also told of an incident that occurred with one of her staff members, Mary Eben. Her secretary had passed the Lincoln bedroom one day and noticed a tall, thin man who was sitting on the edge of the bed, pulling on a pair of boots. She then realized that the figure was Abraham Lincoln! As the late president had been dead for about 75 years at the time, she was understandably frightened and she ran screaming back to her office. Mary became just one of the many people who saw Lincoln's ghost during FDR's time in the White House, including the President's valet, who once ran out of the mansion, shrieking in fear that he had just seen Abraham Lincoln.

In addition to the residents and staff members of the White House, a number of notable visitors also encountered Lincoln during this time. One story relates to Queen Wilhelmina of the Netherlands, who spent the night in the White House during the War years, while in exile from the Nazis. It was said that she was sleeping in the Rose Room when she heard an insistent tapping on the door. As the hour was quite late, she assumed the summons must be important and she quickly opened the door. There, standing in the doorway, was Abraham Lincoln!

According to a White House staff member, the Queen surprised President Franklin D. Roosevelt, and a number of cocktail party guests, the next evening when she recalled her encounter. She told them that after seeing the apparition, everything went black and she later woke up on the floor. By this time, the ghost had vanished.

The late British Prime Minister Winston Churchill never discussed Lincoln's ghost, but many believe that he may have encountered him while visiting the White House. Churchill was always quartered in the Lincoln Bedroom during his stays, as were all visiting male heads of state, but the next morning, he would normally be found sleeping in a room across the hall. He confessed that he never felt comfortable in that particular room but refused to discuss what made him so fearful of it.

Of all of the presidents who encountered Lincoln's ghost, the best known was President Harry S. Truman, who made no bones about the fact that he believed the White House to be haunted. He once recalled an incident that took place in the early morning hours, about one year after he took office. He was awakened that night by knocking on his bedroom door. He got out of bed, went to the door and opened it, but found that no one was in the hallway. Suddenly, the air around him felt icy cold but the chill quickly faded as President Truman heard the sound of footsteps moving away from him down the corridor.

He later wrote to his wife, Bess, who often stayed at their family home in Missouri because she didn't like Washington, that "I sit in this old house, all the while listening to the ghosts walk up and down the hallway. At four o'clock, I was awakened by three distinct knocks on my bedroom door. No one was there.

)amned place is haunted, sure as shootin'!"

During his time in office, President Dwight D. Eisenhower made no effort to leny the experiences that he'd had with Lincoln's ghost. He told his press secreary, James Haggerty, that he frequently sensed Lincoln's ghost in the White House. One day, he explained that he was walking down a hallway when approaching him from the opposite direction was the figure of Abraham Lincoln. Eisenhower took the encounter in stride --- after the horrors of war, the specter of Lincoln was probably a welcome sight. Surprisingly, Haggerty told of he President's ghostly experience on a network television program, despite the ong-held White House position on a strict "no ghost" policy.

Jacqueline Kennedy, who occupied the White House with her family and husband, John F. Kennedy, exactly 100 years after the Lincoln's lived there, admitted that she sensed Lincoln's presence in the mansion. Although there is no record of President Kennedy ever encountering the ghost, Jackie told reporters in 1961 that she found the White House to be "cold and drab" and disliked much of the furnishings. With this in mind, she undertook a major renovation. When she had completed the widely publicized refurbishment, the White House was freshly painted and redecorated. This is when Lincoln's ghost began to stir again. Likely, he was unsettled by the massive alterations in the house and it was during the restoration that Jackie began to encounter his ghost. When he occupied the White House, Lincoln paid little attention to the furnishings and once was very angry with Mary when she spent too much money decorating "this damned old house".

Despite official denials, members of the first families continued to encounter Lincoln's specter. When Gerald Ford was in office, his daughter, Susan, publicly acknowledged her belief in ghosts and made it clear that she would never sleep in the Lincoln Bedroom - or "that room", as she called it. According to one account, Susan actually witnessed Lincoln's spirit.

The late President Ronald Reagan even mentioned Lincoln's ghost in a 1987 press conference. He told the reporters who were gathered that he was never frightened by the spirit. "I haven't seen him myself," Reagan said, "but every once in a while our little dog Rex will start down that long hall, just glaring as though he's seeing something." He also added that the dog would bark repeatedly as he stopped in front of the Lincoln bedroom. Reagan said that if he opened the door to the bedroom and tried to get the dog to come inside, Rex would growl fiercely but refused to step over the threshold.

There were no reports of Lincoln's ghost during the Bush administration and both the President and Mrs. Bush denied seeing Lincoln or any other ghost in the White House. However, during the Clinton years, there were at least two sightings of Lincoln's apparition. One encounter was admitted by President Clinton's brother, Roger, who stated that he had sensed Lincoln's presence in the

White House. In the second instance, a Clinton aide admitted that he had seen Lincoln walking down a hallway but the story, which was briefly reported in the news, was quickly denied and dismissed by the White House as a joke. As of this writing, no reports of Lincoln's ghost have filtered out of White House concerning the current President, George W. Bush, but who knows what stories will be told in the years to come.

So does the ghost of Abraham Lincoln really walk in the White House?

Some of our country's most influential leaders have certainly believed so. But why does he still walk here? Is the apparition merely a faded memory of another time or an actual presence? Does the ghost appear, as has been suggested, during times of crisis, when perhaps the assistance of the president who faced America's greatest crisis is most needed?

President Harry Truman had no idea why Lincoln's ghost was still present in the White House. In her biography about the president, Margaret Truman stated that her father certainly had no ambitions to haunt the White House himself.

"No man in his right mind would want to come here of his own accord," he said.

BIBLIOGRAPHY & RECOMMENDED READING

Alexander, John - Ghosts: Washington's Greatest Ghost Stories (1975)
Angle, Paul - Here I Have Lived: A History of Lincoln's Springfield (1935)
Bielski, Ursula - Chicago Haunts (1998)
Bishop, Jim - The Day Lincoln was Shot (1955)
Blue & Gray Magazine - Guide to Haunted Places of the Civil War (1996)
Donald, David Herbert - Lincoln (1995)
Evans, C. Wyatt - The Legend of John Wilkes Booth (2004)
Gallagher, Trish - Ghosts & Haunted House of Maryland (1988)
Garrison, Webb - The Lincoln No One Knows (1993)
Guttridge, Leonard F. & Ray A. Neff - Dark Union (2003)
Hanchett, William - The Lincoln Murder Conspiracies (1983)
Hauck, Dennis William - Haunted Places: The National Directory (1996)
Higham, Charles - Murdering Mr. Lincoln (2004)
Jameson, W.C. - Unsolved Mysteries of the Old West (1999)
Kunhardt, Dorothy Meserve & Phillip Kunhardt Jr. - Twenty Days (1965)
Kunhardt, Phillip B. Jr, Phillip Kunhardt III & Peter Kunhardt - Lincoln
    (1992)
Lewis, Loyd - Myths After Lincoln (1929)
Life Magazine
Martinb, Joel & William J. Birnes - The Haunting of the Presidents (2003)
Maynard, Nettie Colburn - Was Abraham Lincoln a Spiritualist? ((1917)
Mogelever, Jacob - Death to Traitors (1960)
Oates, Stephen B. - With Malice Toward None (1977)
Rainey, Richard - Haunted History (1989)
Roscoe, Theodore - The Web of Conspiracy (1959)
Speer, Bonnie Stahlman - Great Abraham Lincoln Hijack (1990)
Springfield State Journal- Register (Newspaper)
Steers, Edward, Jr. - Blood on the Moon (2001)
Stern, Phillip Van Doren - The Man Who Killed Lincoln (1939)
Taylor, Troy - Ghosts of Springfield (1997)
Taylor, Troy - Haunted Chicago (2003)
Taylor, Troy - Haunted Illinois (2004)
Taylor, Troy - Spirits of the Civil War (1999)
Trostel, Scott D. - The Lincoln Funeral Train (2002)

Vankin, Jonathan & John Whalen - 70 Greatest Conspiracies of All Time (1998)
Walker, Dale - Legends & Lies: Great Mysteries of the American West (1997)
Walsh, John Evangelist - Moonlight (2000)
Weichmann, Louis J. - The True History of the Assassination of Abraham Lincoln and the Conspiracy of 1865 (1975)
Winer, Richard & Nancy Osborn Ishmael - More Haunted Houses (1981)
Winkler, H. Donald - Lincoln and Booth (2003)
Winterbauer, John - Stealing Abraham Lincoln (Ghosts of the Prairie 2003)
Winterbauer, John - Ghosts of Route 66: New Salem (Ghosts of the Prairie 2004)

Personal Interviews and Correspondence

Special Thanks to:
Kim Young - Proofreading & Editing Services
John Winterbauer
and Ursula Bielski

ABOUT THE AUTHOR - TROY TAYLOR

Troy Taylor is the author of 35 books about history, hauntings and the unexplained in America, including HAUNTED ILLINOIS, HAUNTED CHICAGO, WEIRD ILLINOIS and many others. He is also the editor of GHOSTS OF THE PRAIRIE Magazine, about the history, hauntings & unsolved mysteries of America. A number of his articles have been published here and in other publications.

Along with writing about the unusual, Taylor is also a public speaker on the subject and has spoken to literally hundreds of private and public groups on a variety of paranormal subjects. He has appeared in newspaper and magazine articles about ghosts and hauntings. He has also been fortunate enough to be interviewed hundreds of times for radio and television broadcasts about the supernatural. He has also appeared in a number of documentary films, several television series and in one feature film.

Born and raised in Illinois, Taylor has long had an affinity for "things that go bump in the night" and published his first book in 1995. For seven years, he was also the host of the popular, and award-winning, "Haunted Decatur" ghost tours of the city for which he sometimes still appears as a guest host. He also hosted tours in St. Louis and St. Charles, Missouri, as well as in Alton and Chicago, Illinois. Along with fellow author and writing partner Ursula Bielski, he is also co-owner of the Bump in the Night Tour Co., which hosts overnight excursions to haunted places throughout the Midwest.

He currently resides in Central Illinois in a decidedly non-haunted house.

ABOUT WHITECHAPEL PRODUCTIONS PRESS

Whitechapel Productions Press is a small press publisher, specializing in books about ghosts and hauntings. Since 1993, the company has been one of America's leading publishers of supernatural books. Located in Decatur, Illinois, they also produce the "Ghosts of the Prairie" Internet web page and "Ghosts of the Prairie", a print magazine that is dedicated to American hauntings and unsolved mysteries.

In addition to publishing books and the periodical on history and hauntings, Whitechapel Press also owns and distributes the Haunted America Catalog, which features over 700 different books about ghosts and hauntings from authors all over the United States. A complete selection of these books on our Internet website.

Visit Whitechapel Productions Press online and browse through our selection of ghostly titles, plus get information on ghosts and hauntings, haunted history, spirit photographs, information on ghost hunting and much more.

Visit the Internet web page at:

www.historyandhauntings.com

Whitechapel Press is also connected to the acclaimed History & Hauntings Ghost Tours of Alton, Illinois, which were created by Troy Taylor. The tours are an interactive experience that allow readers to visit the historically haunted locations of the city and can be booked between April and July and in October. We are also home to Troy Taylor & Ursula Bielski's Bump in the Night Ghost Tour Co., which offers Haunted Overnight Excursions to ghostly places around the Midwest and throughout the country.

Information on our books and tours are available on the website.

UPCOMING TITLES FROM WHITECHAPEL PRESS & HAUNTED ILLINOIS

DEAD MEN DO TELL TALES
History & Hauntings of Illinois Crime
by Ursula Bielski & Troy Taylor

GHOSTS BY GASLIGHT
History, Hauntings & Hoaxes of American Spiritualism
by Troy Taylor & Ursula Bielski

MYSTERIOUS ILLINOIS
Strange Events, Weird Places & Unsolved Mysteries of Illinois
by Troy Taylor

ILLINOIS HAUNTINGS
The Travel Guide to Haunted Illinois
by Troy Taylor, Ursula Bielski & Michael Schwab

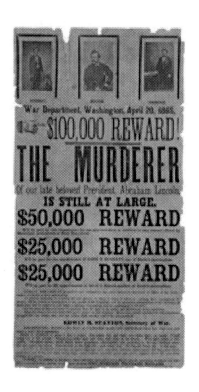

Printed in the United States
60689LVS00001B/250-261